POLITICAL LEADERSHIP

And

AFRICAN WOMEN

With a Focus on West Africa

Amadou Beidy Sow

Book Vine Press
2516 Highland Dr.
Palatine, IL 60067

CONTENTS

• •

ABBREVIATIONS
•••

KTN	Kenya Television Network
AOF/FWA	*Afrique Occidentale Française/* French West Africa
RDA	African Democratic Rally
PSP	Progressive Party of Sudan
US-RDA	African Democratic Rally-Sudanese-Union
USF	Union of Sudanese Women
UFOA	Women's Union of West Africa
UNFM	*Union Nationale des Femmes du Mali*
NUMW	National Union of Malian Women
ARWAW	African Renaissance of West African Women
RAFAO	*Africaine des Femmes d'Afrique de l'Ouest*

UNESCO	United Nations Educational, Scientific and Cultural Organization
MCNL	Military Committee of National Liberation
CNID	National Congress of Democratic Initiative
ADEMA	Alliance for Democracy in Mali
AMDH	Malian Association of Human Rights
CTSP	Transition Committee for the Salvation of the People
CNID-*FYT*	National Congress of Democratic Initiative – *Faso Yiriwa Ton*
ADEMA-PASJ	Alliance for Democracy in Mali – African Party for Solidarity
UNDP	United Nations Development Program
PROWWESS	Promotion of the Role of Women in Water and Environmental Sanitation Services
ADVR	Association for the Defense of Victims of Repression called
CFA	*Communaute Financiere Africaine* (African Financial Community)
ABANTU	From Zulu umuntu (plural abantu) human being, person

PREFACE

It would be appealing to see leaders providing leadership rather than paying attention to constituencies, groups, communities, professions, interests or gender. One should say without any reluctance that women are the pillars of a society or a country, and any act that leads to the preparation of women for these roles in taking leadership positions, should be valued. When we give the chance to cogitate on people that have been the heart and the mind of their family or community, women would be seen at the forefront. And they can do much more if they are given the chance, the trust, and the support they need within their communities. Women in African countries are left behind in political decision-making whereas their participation could bring about tremendous change. Although politics has historically been considered to be the past time and the domain of men, women have always contributed to political affairs despite their absence on the political sphere. This absence of women is explained here by their number and not by their physical presence because women have historically played political leadership roles as queens. This physical presence of women in politics can also be argued according to certain political analysts. One has to simply observe how many different organizations are working to encourage women's political participation throughout the world and the tremendous effort they are using in order to achieve this goal.

Generally, the majority of women in Africa are present and are visible at the grassroots level, but are not allowed to be active in the decision-making level because of their lack of political leadership roles. Women are still not benefiting from the system in spite of the fact that they have the desire and energy to be at the forefront of the decision-making process similar to men who are in politics. Conversely, the argument is neither to bring women in mass in politics nor to leave political activities entirely in the hands of women. In fact, if there is a concern regarding the absence of women in political leadership positions, it will be also interesting to know what direction such a leadership might take. It is significant to understand the real motives of international organizations in their quest for women's participation in the political activities within their own society. If people know the hardship that women face getting into politics, how much do they know about the leadership of women who are already in politics?

Insofar as this work addresses African women's political leadership being the center, this study presents a prototype of leadership that can be applicable to other societies and groups. This work is neither based on the comparison between women and men as political leaders nor is it concerned about any specific woman politician. It focuses on women who are involved in politics in Africa, especially in Mali. It examines the social, religious, economic, political, and educational experiences of women who are political leaders.

INTRODUCTION

This book is based on the political leadership styles of women in a society that has for a long time been the heart and the pillar of the Manding[1] civilization, the center of its knowledge and the gate to the outside world through Timbuktu and Djenne (Jenne)[2]. This civilization has been strongly influenced by the presence of the Arab values over a century hence their way of dealing with political affairs and European values. Even though Mali had its own way of dealing with the affairs of the state which cannot be denied, it is important to notice that what prevails today is the western model in this context blended with the one on the ground, especially in Mali. This same European presence in Africa has contributed to the oppression of women and hindered their social and political integration. Even though women made their debut in politics during the Europeans'

---

[1] Manding was an empire in West Africa created around XI Century by Sunjata Keita and became renowned for the wealth of its rulers especially Musa Keita (Mansa Musa).

[2] Djenne/Jenne, one of the oldest known cities in sub-Saharan Africa is located in the central part of Mali. It is known as a business and religious center. The famous mosque of Djenne was built according to the tradition in 1240 by the Sultan Koi Kunboro, who converted to Islam and turned his palace into a mosque.

colonial oppressive rule, it must be clarified that the presence of those women in politics was the work of African Nationalists. African Nationalists had been on the forefront of women's emancipation and inspiration on the political scene that had been denied to them for a long time. Thus, this work will deal with the role of women and their political history in the past and present, how women see politics in social, economic and religious standpoints. It will further observe the economic power of women, the impact of modern education on woman vis-à-vis politics and what woman politicians do with power once in the political leadership position. This work will talk about what leadership is in its different contexts. The first chapter analyzes women's roles in different times in their society. It also highlights young girls' education. The second chapter focuses on the aim of colonial schools in the colonies in general, and in the French Sudan and its impacts on women in the present day. The third chapter discusses the historical context of women political debut and the role played by certain key figures in politics in order to better understand their progress. The fourth chapter looks at a particular case about women involvement in political leadership positions and the roles they played in those different governments. The fifth chapter analyzes women's role in politics and their opinion about political leadership, which indirectly helps understand the type of leadership they try to display on the political scene.

What is Leadership

There are several definitions of leadership, but there still remains a lack of clarity regarding tangible distinctions between leaders and non-leaders[3]. Leadership theorists have categorized different aspects of leadership that influence teacher-politicians' leadership characteristics. In essence, there is little consensus among the theorists[4].

---

[3]   Bennis, W. G., & Nanus, B. (1997). Leaders: Strategies for taking Charge, (2nd ed.).

[4]   Burns J. M. (1978). Leadership. New York, N.Y: Harper & Row.; Bennis, W. G., & Nanus, B. (1997). Leaders: Strategies for taking Charge, (2nd ed.).; Bass, B. M. (1990). Bass & Stogdill's handbook of leadership. New York, NY: The Free.

Despite this lack of consensus regarding the characteristic of leadership, the different theorists have shed more light about the phenomenon of leadership. However, the majority of the researchers examined leadership from two perspectives, transformational and transactional[5]. While some leadership theorists such as Burns and Palestini divide leadership between top down and bottom up[6]. Birch argues that all leadership is top down[7]. Popper asserts that followers have the same impact on leaders as leaders have on followers[8]. Bennis and Nanus analyze a new theory of leadership, specifically leadership in a managerial context. They insist that, over the years leadership has changed and has given birth to a new theory, nevertheless, the competencies of leaders have remained the same[9]. Leaders have always acted the same way and have not demonstrated new competencies.

Leadership according to House "the ability of an individual to influence, motivate, and enable others to contribute toward the effectiveness and success of the organizations of which they are members"[10]. For Burns, a leader is not someone who simply handles power, but someone who also appreciates the values of the

---

[5]   Bass, B. M. (1985). Leadership and performance beyond expectation. New York, NY: Free Press.; Foster, W. P. (1989). Towards a critical practice of leadership. In J. Smythe (Ed.), Critical perspectives on leadership, (pp. 39-62). London, UK: Falmer Press.; Palestini, R. H. (2003). The human touch in educational leadership: A postpositivist approach to understanding educational leadership. Boston, MA: Rowman & Littlefield Publishers, Inc.; Rost, J. C. (1991). Leadership for the twenty-first century. (1st ed.). New York, NY: Praeger.; Tierney, W.G. (1989). Advancing democracy: A critical interpretation of leadership. Peabody Journal of Education, 66(3), 157-175.; Wolfenstein, E.V. (1967). The revolutionary personality: Lenin, Trotsky, Ghandi. (1st ed.). Princeton, NJ: Princeton University Press.; Burns J. M. (1978). Leadership. New York, N.Y: Harper & Row.

[6]   Burns J. M. (1978). Leadership. New York, N.Y: Harper & Row.; Palestini, R. H. (2003). The human touch in educational leadership: A postpositivist approach to understanding educational leadership. Boston, MA: Rowman & Littlefield Publishers, Inc.

[7]   (1999) Birch, P. (1999). Instant leadership. London: Kogan Page.

[8]   Popper, M. (2005). Leaders who transform society. Westport, CT: Praeger/Greenwood.

[9]   Popper, M. (2005). Leaders who transform society. Westport, CT: Praeger/Greenwood.

[10] House, R. J. (2004). Culture, leadership, and organizations: The globe study of 62 societies. Thousand Oaks, CA: Sage Publications. p15

constituency. He continues by discussing that some people describe a leader as someone who makes followers do what he or she wishes them to do. This attitude affects the credibility of a leader. In addition, the credibility of leaders is very important. Once a person accepts a leadership position and assumes the responsibilities of a leader, the person abandons privacy[11].

Despite the recent work of 'social psychologists' and 'organizational theorists', there is no complete description of the complex phenomenon of leadership. People have different meanings for a leader and leadership. This situation may be because of the confusion about the definition and agreement about the meaning of the key terms. Furthermore, the absence of a common language explains why the phenomenon is less explored[12]. Leaders are supposed to serve as models, symbols, and representatives of their people[13]. Leadership is not only the role played by a single individual but also the relationship between leaders and their constituencies[14].

Leadership can include the relationship between people that guides them toward a collective vision or goal. In the same vein, Rost discusses the difference between leadership and any from or sort of management[15]. In the Republic, Plato defines leadership in three ways. First, leaders are philosopher-statesmen who govern the republic with rationality and fairness. Second, they are military commanders who protect the state and put into action its will. Third, leaders are businessmen, who supply citizens' substance needs. This argument of Plato is the proof of the applicability of leadership in different social contexts. Leadership may be argued as a process of opinion by which a person persuades his/her constituency to pursue so that certain objectives can be met[16].

---

[11]   Bennis, W. G., & Nanus, B. (1997). Leaders: Strategies for taking Charge, (2nd ed.)

[12]   Kellerman, B. (Ed.). (1984). Leadership: Multidisciplinary perspectives. Englewood Cliffs, NJ: Prentice-Hall.

[13]   Bass, B. M. (1990). Bass & Stogdill's handbook of leadership. New York, NY: The Free.

[14]   Rost, 1991Rost, J. C. (1991). Leadership for the twenty-first century. (1st ed.). New York, NY: Praeger.

[15]   Rost, J. C. (1991). Leadership for the twenty-first century. (1st ed.). New York, NY: Praeger.

[16]   (Gardner, 1990). Gardner, W. J. (1990). On leadership. New York, NY: Free Press.

Leaders assist organizations to build up new visions of what they can be. Another position is that leaders commit group to action, converting constituencies into leaders, which in turn motivate these new leaders to become actors of change[17]. Leaders and followers are not two antagonist forces[18]. They complete each other. In addition, if the goal of education is to help individuals to reach an objective, those who lead need to consider their respective roles. They continue saying that leadership can be the pivotal power sustaining booming organizations. It can also have the capability of building crucial and realistic organizations. For Popper, Leadership is a dynamic relationship including leaders and followers. Mencius suggests that the leadership conferred to a person can be taken away if he/she fails to lead with the 'moral command of heaven'[19]. It is evident on the political scene women will try to display transactional leadership or transactional or leadership that might help to understand their social and political life.

---

[17] Burns J. M. (1978). Leadership. New York, N.Y: Harper & Row.; Palestini, R. H. (2003). The human touch in educational leadership: A postpositivist approach to understanding educational leadership. Boston, MA: Rowman & Littlefield Publishers, Inc.; Popper, M. (2005). Leaders who transform society. Westport, CT: Praeger/Greenwood.

[18] Bennis, W. G., & Nanus, B. (1997). Leaders: Strategies for taking Charge, (2nd ed.)

[19] Mencius. (1970). Mencius. Translated by Lau. D. C. England, St Ives: Clays ltd.

CHAPTER I

●●

WOMEN'S SOCIAL AND POLITICAL LIFE

This chapter analyzes women's roles in different periods in their society. The role African women have played in the past and the path to their schooling. It will also be highlighting the type of schooling that was put in place for women. Historically, African women have played an important role in many traditional societies. In Mali, there was a lady called Nyeleni[20]. She was a very strong woman that symbolized the sovereignty of women and their social struggle. She was a great woman who has gone into history of Mali as a lady, a remarkable

---

[20] **Nyeleni** represents a brave woman in the Malian society. Nyéléni was a legendary Bamanan peasant woman who farmed and fed her people well – she incarnates food sovereignty through hard work, innovation, and caring.

farmer. The name Nyeleni in Mali, mainly in the Bamanan[21] society, represents a foster mother, a great farmer, who fought to assert herself as a woman in an environment that was not favorable to women. Nyéléni was a single child, which was a curse in the Manding society . Nyéléni, a single child of her parents, suffered in her youth from all kinds of mockeries of which her parents were the cause. Nyeleni's secret resolution was from her desire to wash the affront of men by beating them on their own ground, in agriculture and the works of the land. Any pretender who wanted to marry her, she kept repeating that it could wait, that she had first a mission to accomplish, to pay a tribute back to her family, to the woman and to all the women and that this was her priority. Nyeleni, at the agricultural competitions, was the pawn of all known and renowned champions in her village and surrounding villages. She became well-known and her reputation grew and grew. The most arrogant men defied the champion all day long. Unfortunately for them, she defeated everyone. Nyeleni's reputation transcended the borders of her country, she had become a living myth. At that time, fame was built and respected. The legend reports that it was Nyeleni who domesticated the fonio grain.

Likewise, in Egypt, women played significant roles in the government of their country. An example is Queen Hatshepsut, who with her brother ruled ancient Egypt. This Queen is believed to have expanded Egypt due to her architectural talent. She was also known as a businesswoman who went to modern Sudan in search of trade. She was believed to be the real power behind the throne as was the Queen Mother in Ghana. In Nigeria, two famous women played important roles in the political and social life of their country, Amina of Zaria and Madam Tinubu in Southern Nigeria. The famous Amina of Zaria was believed to have built the city walls of Zaria and ruled an empire in the Northern part of the country in the 16e century.

---

[21] **Bamanan** are members of the Mande culture, a large and powerful group of peoples in western Africa. Kaarta and Segou are the main Bamana city-states. The Kingdom was ruled by the Kulubali or Coulibaly dynasty established c. 1640 by Kaladian Kulubali and then ruled by the Jara Jara dynasty. The mud cloth/*bogolan* was invented by the Bamana people which plays a key role in the society.

There was also Madam Tinubu who was essentially a businesswoman dealing with salt, tobacco and slaves. She made her incursion into politics when in 1846 the King of Lagos, Agba Akitoye was deposed. Madam Tinubu backed Akitoye and in 1851 restored him to the throne. She was banished to Abeokuta because she was instrumental to the strong political influence, which made her a threat by the Lagos elites, and she was also engaged in the arms business. During the war between the Agba and the Dahomey, Madam Tinubu supplied arms to the Agba in 1864. This action of Madam Tinubu contributed to the defeat of the Dahomey by Agba and for this, Madam Tinubu was rewarded with the prestigious title of Iyalode[22] which gave her a voice in Agba politics. Despite the status of men in most of the African societies, little was known about Madam Tinubu's husband. She was believed to have been given a state burial on her death.

In Guinea-Bissau, Queen Juliana led a rebellion against the Portuguese colonialists and was finally conquered. In Nigeria, the women of Agba rioted protesting colonial oppression. Many African women also took part in the struggle for independence. In post-colonial Africa, with many countries gaining their independence, most African countries adopted the system of universal adult suffrage and in most cases, the parliamentary systems of their colonizers. Whilst these systems should have worked to the advantage of women, it put them at a further disadvantage. The cause of this is that political parties were formed by men and had little room for women. Although many women had by now acquired an education, few could boast of being educated at the same level as their male counterparts. The women who were taking part in the struggle for independence found that they were marginalized when it came to the field for parliamentary seats or political appointments. In order to appease these women, some political parties devised the instrument of the women's wings. In most cases, women's wings were formed to provide entertainment and refreshments at the campaign rallies of

---

[22] **Iyalode** is a chieftaincy title commonly bestowed on women in Yorubaland. Traditionally, the Iyalode signifies the "queens of ladies" and is given to the most prominent and distinguished lady in or from the town.

the men and of course to mobilize other women to vote for the men. These women's wings were reduced to singing, dancing and clapping instruments to boost the political campaigns of the men.

The Role of Women in Pre-Modern Society

African women have played major roles in their society throughout the history of the continent even though they were first limited to aspects such as the management of domestic affairs, social life and artisan workshops. The part played by African women, particularly Malian women, in their social life needs to be paid special attention. This contribution of women in their society should be analyzed in the past and the present context in order to have a clear understanding of what women represent for their people today. It is difficult to deny the significant roles women have played and continue to play today in the African society. This role is not only restricted to Malian women, but to the majority of African women as a whole. In order to understand these roles played by women in Africa in the past and the present time, it will become sine qua non to observe women in their different times in the African societies.

The functions of African women, mainly Malian women, in the traditional society has been for a long time limited to the daily management of domestic affairs and artisan workshops. At the 7th Annual Trust Dialogue in Abuja, Kofo Bucknor-Akerele, a Nigerian Senator, stated that, "Historically the African woman's place has always been in the home to nurture the family and give birth to children. In many African societies, the children should be seen and not heard. In this instance, we can change the word children for women. In some societies, women were not even seen let alone heard.'[23] Bucknor-Akele displayed the tremendous skills of women in these fields that are manifold. Besides the traditional responsibility of women as housewives, they are at the same time farmers in the field, artisans in mud cloth and pottery, and vendors in the market. Both political and

---

[23]   The 7th Annual Trust Dialogue that was held in Abuja, Nigeria on January 21, 2010

religious power in traditional Malian society is exercised by the elders that can be women or men. Even though the majority of these powers remain in the hands of men, women still play leadership roles. Women were not landlords *dugukolotiw* or chief of village *dugutigi*, but they enjoy leadership, *kuntigiya*, as well as men.

According to historical contingencies, the leader can appoint heads of districts and delegate some of its administrative powers. The authority of cult leaders is also important. But they work closely with the village chief who is also the one that traditionally authorizes the practice of any religion in his village. Women in the traditional society have enjoyed their leadership roles within organizations or associations in many African societies such as *tɔnw* in Mali. However, if women have enjoyed authority within certain African societies, it would be also interesting to know that this was not the case for all of the ethnic groups in Mali nor for Africa. The So[24] in northern Cameroon also tell of myths in which women regularly chose the site where a settlement would be established. The same So women in northern Cameroon held major political positions in their community and could choose the place where a village would be established. More importantly, they could be responsible for the leadership of a district. Kofo Bucknor-Akerele indicated that "Queen Hatchepsut in ancient Egypt, queen of Shiba modern Ethiopia, Amina of Saria in Nigeria, Queen mother of Ghana, Queen Kanyimpa in Guinea-Bissau, Nyeleni in Mali played important role in their respective countries as leaders." Referring to Kofo's argument, it sheds light on the role played by women on the political scene even though this role is for the most part limited to a monarchical dimension of leadership. The monarchical leaders with women as leaders started going underground with the presence of the French colonial oppressive force in the newly occupied territories in Africa. Women started losing the authority that before remained in their hands due to outside conquest or dominance. During that period, women were in charge of domestic duties, as it was the same in their

---

[24]   Falola, T., Amponsah, N. A. (2012). Women's Roles in Sub-Saharan Africa.ABC/
       CLIO. P155

countries, before they started to surface on the public scene with the creation of schools.

The Role of Woman during the Colonial Epoch

The colonial epoch, for the first time, kept women away from any social participation and later on brought them back with the creation of school in the public sphere. In order to understand the role of women during the colonial oppression, it becomes important to refer to what Paulo Freire called the relationship between the oppressed and the oppressor[25]. It is without any ambiguity to say that the relationship between the oppressed and the oppressor has very often benefited one and oppressed the other. Women under the colonial administration, even in certain African societies, were not benefiting from certain privileges. The argument of Barthelemy demonstrates that colonialism did not give the same chance to African women as African men for their political, economic and social fulfillment. Women were kept away from the public sphere, keeping them under male domination. Barthelemy.[26] In addition, the French administration subordinated African women by force and it also revealed that this type of subordination of women existed in some African societies. These injustices to African women during the colonial era encouraged them to stand up for themselves and their families. There are different events in Africa that support this struggle and the hardship of women.

The role of Malian women is partly discussed by the role Amadou H. Ba's mother played when her husband was arrested by the French colonial administration and sentenced to total seclusion. This type of woman has always been considered as a *Nyeleni* in the Bamanan society. Today this refers to any woman that distinguishes herself in the society by her courage, hard work, contribution to her community, and dedication as the Bamanan woman called *Nyeleni*. Due to the role she played in the fight against the French

---

[25] Paulo Freire, Pedagogy of the Oppressed, 30th Anniversary Edition. 2000.

[26] P. Barthelemy (2010). *Africaines et diplômées à l'époque coloniale (1918-1957)*

establishment, Kadidia becomes a *Nyeleni*. She, after receiving the news of the deportation of her husband to a secluded prison, tried to use her competence to be close to her husband. This was an unthinkable act at that time, to negotiate with the French colonial administration. After Kadidia's tete-a-tete with the French colonial administrator under recommendation of a colonial interpreter, the colonial administrator responded in these terms:

> I do not have the power to authorize anyone to accompany Tidjani Thiam because, as you know, he was sentenced to total seclusion and his cadi Tierno Kunta Cisse. No visits, no support is therefore allowed. However, if one was held on the facts of the accusation, both should have been sentenced to death or to seclusion perpetuate, but I have considered, in the judgment of certain circumstances I discovered and even made me forget that Tidjani, in a kind of access of despair, failed to kill me I myself on the road, as if to prevent me to come to his rescue. So I cannot allow you to go with him. However, I cannot prevent anyone to make a trip from Bougouni to Bandiagara. The road is wide open. Just ask for official pass.[27]

The audience of Kadidia with the district commander was to facilitate the sentence of her husband. Kadidia's presence in Bougouni aimed to become a physical and moral support to her husband. She also symbolized in her fight for her husband a dedicated woman ready to sacrifice her own freedom and wealth. It is important to understand that Kadidia was a successful and wealthy woman, and she financed her trip to Bougouni by selling many of her cattle (source of wealth in the Fulani's society).

The role of women observed in the optic of the colonial administration was nothing compared to what women experienced in their former societies. There is not the Bamanan or Dogon

---

[27] Amadou H. Ba, (1984). *Amkoullel, l'enfant peul [The Fulani child]*. France: Actes Sud. 1992. p134

woman who would disagree with me. This argument of Mme de Noirfontaine best describes the miserable destiny of Africans, mainly its women, who are the focus of this study. "The future of Africa...is decided in administrations and by people who know little of it and whose main purpose is to exploit the place in any way they can."[28] Gender inequality has been one of those tangible tools used by the French and the British, in the territories under their control, to exploit Africa. One of the tools used by these forces in the dominated territories was to emphasize gender inequality bringing the sole men on the forefront reinforcing their power in the society. It is important to point out that the Islamic religion has changed the role of women, reinforced or even worsened by the French colonial administration. It is also important to discuss the role played by women during the colonial era even though it seems that women were not visible during this time. The French colonial laws at first never educated women and were concerned about the education of men to serve what they called the colonial administration. Administrators were trained in the Colonial School.

These two new forces together diminished women's political activities reducing their roles to a mere household occupation. In the African countries under their domination, it was only French men who were serving in the colonial administration.[29] Rosaldo & al explain the shared role between men and women in the territories dominated by the French in these terms: "In most societies the world of the domestic and familial is the world of women, and that of the public and political the world of men."[30] In the new African territories conquered by France, French men were for a long time not allowed to bring their wives and these men were allowed to marry African women, hence colonial marriage. The irony in these marriages were

---

[28]   Volet, 2007Jean-Marie Volet 2007. Women's perception of French colonial life in 19th century Africa: a fascinating universe challenging conventional. Retrieved 9/26/2011 from wisdomhttp://aflit.arts.uwa.edu.au/colonies 19e eng.html Troubles post-électoraux, Afrique express N° 152,11 septembre 1997

[29]   Bâ, A. H. (1984). Amkoullel, l'enfant peul [Amkoullel The Fulani child]. France: Actes Sud.

[30]   Rosaldo, M. Z; Lamphere, L; Bamberger, J. (1974). Woman, culture, and society. Stanford University Press.

that these marriages celebrated in the African territories under the French colonial domination did not have any value before the French law back home. French men in these territories were forced to divorce their wives or leave them to the person who was taking over their position when their service ended. In certain cases, a man could leave behind a little wealth or allowance to the children[31]. Moreover, it took a while before the law allowed French women to go with their husbands in the new territories based on different reasons. The first was to make a great impression among Africans and the second reason was due to the hostile images presented to them about Africans and their natural environment. However, the arrival of French women in the conquered territories opened the way to girls' education.

It was toward the end of the French colonial oppressive rule in the country that women started going to school to become teachers and nurses (sage femmes). We have to elucidate that during that time French schools opened their doors to accept women, and because of religious reasons parents were skeptical of sending their daughters to schools, even though it was compulsory. Despite colonial oppression, some women happened to join the political scene during the colonial era.[32]

Philosophy Behind Women Schooling

African women's schooling is deeply rooted in numerous reasons in their respective societies, which also helps to understand their challenges in politics. The philosophy behind women's schooling could be ingrained in cultural, economic, religious and colonial causes. Even though certain people argue in favor of traditional education, it is to some level considered by certain researchers an obstacle to girls' schooling. According to Amadou Hampate Ba, girls' parents were not in favor of sending their daughters to school because they believed it would inculcate in them foreign culture in

---

[31] Maryse Conde (1988). *Segu*. Ballantine publication.
[32] Amponsah, N. A., Falola. T (2012). *Women's Roles in Sub-Saharan Africa*. Greenwood Publication. Santa Barbara, California

one way. In another way, girls were expected to keep the tradition alive and pass it on to the next generation to come. Furthermore, if the father is expected to educate the young boys, the same role is played by the young girls' mother. Mothers are responsible for the education of their girls. The fact of separating the young girl from her mother that she grows in her shadow, and sends her to school interrupts the role the mother has to play in her daughter's life. Even though this separation of the young girl, to send her to school, is seen as beneficial to her and the family she is going to build in the future. "In the house the woman's education has greater effect on the family."[33] In most of the African societies, girls help their mothers in growing vegetables and selling goods in order to feed the family. The same source went further by arguing that young girls' education can help them to become more successful in the market and on the farm.

In addition to the participation of girls alongside their mothers in feeding the family, today the cost of school fees does not encourage girls' education. Parents prefer to send young boys to school that will continue the family heritage while young girls will be married in another family living in their father's house. Another reason, as supported by Hampate Ba, is that young girls' low literacy rate is based on the fact that most of the parents believe that sending a young girl to school will help her embrace the western values, hence Christianity. This attitude of parents could be explained by the attitudes of missionaries in the country. Conversely, even though missionaries through the colonial administration started girls' education, this education was only encouraged late and did not help young girls to contribute to their social life. The colonial administration was only interested in sending young boys to school. In addition to education brought by the colonial force in the country, the traditional education had trained women to contribute fully to their family and community life.

On top of the traditional role allocated to women to be the manager of the household and to procreate, Malian women have

---

[33]   King, E.M., Hill, A. M. (1997). *Women's education in developing countries: Barriers, benefits, and policies.* The World Bank. p20.

improved agricultural activities by bringing more personnel to the sector and by bringing more food in the family, which was considered to be a serious gap in families. Today, Malian women's role in society is increasing by their contribution and participation in food production which consolidates their role as providers of the family. However, referring to the Malian custom, it recognizes householders the right to manage the land. The rest of the family members, including women, must settle for a right of access. Like many other societies, agricultural production is collectively within the family, the opportunity for women to gain entrée to land is determined by the customs of the family in a given village or a region, as Ba discussed in 'Amkoullel, The Fulani Child'. In certain cases, it does not matter if you are a woman or a man; the collective farmland makes it difficult for individuals to cultivate the land within the family. However, it is important to explain that women are in a disadvantaged position to negotiate for plots. The relations between women and men are instrumental or a key factor to women's access to natural resources and agricultural land.

Women in Africa have always played key roles in economic, political and social situations. In addition, women in Africa have always constituted the numerical majority of the population. The long experience of African women presented by Amadou Hampate Ba, Leopold Senghor, Camara Laye is an eloquent manifestation that they have always played important roles as an economic and political force that has marked the history of the continent. In Mali, women and men associations or *Waalde* have always worked in a harmonious complicity as explained by the author. The same author explained that:

> The *Waalde*....counted one hundred and fifteen young members of both sexes and it controlled and gave protection to five other younger *Waalde* as well as laying down the law in the whole town. Its members organized ambushes against the *tirailleurs*

[Senegalais]34 and the district guards as well as anyone
employed by the establishment who might attempt to
abuse his powers against the indigenous.[35]

Ba further explains the long presence of women in social
organizations in Mali and their involvement in the decision-making
process. It was not the sole responsibility of men to enshrine the
population against any oppression from the French establishment
in their community, but also the one of women to work in harmony
with their counterpart men to work hand in glove. This statement
shows the early presence of women and their participation in
decision-making in the society even though this presence would
reduce progressively due to several reasons instrumental to the French
policy in the society. The change of women's status will be detailed
in the history of the creation of schools in Mali hence in the French-
speaking Africa.

Women in West Africa have always played key roles alongside
men in the traditional society as it is commonly said in Mali.
Young girls' education in the traditional context was to make them
contributors to their social and political affairs. They have always
participated in the decision making in the Malian society based on
the traditional education which later disappeared. It did not matter
talking about political, cultural, economic and religious reasons;
education was supposed to help women in these domains. Women
in Africa have always been an important part of the society until
the advent of Islam but mainly due to the presence of the French
oppressive administration or direct rule[36] to alienate the people. In
order to understand women education, we need to understand the
history of school creation in Mali, former French Sudan.

---

[34] *Tirailleurs Senegalais* were West African Colonial Army troops who fought for the
French during World War I, World War II. They were Africans recruited from Senegal,
French West Africa and subsequently throughout Western, Central and Eastern Africa.

[35] Ba, A. H. (1999). *The fortunes of Wangrin*. Indiana University Press. p19

[36] Direct colonial rule was a form of the French colonialism that involves the establishment
of a centralized authority within the colonies, which was run by colonial officials. The
native population were excluded from all but the last level of the colonial government.

CHAPTER II

WOMEN AND EDUCATION

History of the Creation of Schools

The main aim of the French colonial schools in the colonies in general and in the French Sudan in particular was to educate students how to read and write in order to serve the French colonial administration hence the French economic interest. Women at that time in the history of the colonial occupation of Africa were nowhere to be seen, let alone spoken about regarding their education, which was not of interest to the colonial administration. The presence of women in the public sphere during the colonial oppression time period is depicted in this section through the creation of school in Africa. The system that regulated the creation of schools in Mali was a common system for all West African countries under the French colonial domination. The French had at the beginning of their colonial occupation in the French Sudan a serious difficulty in communicating with the native people, just like they had anywhere else in the continent. Language being an important tool for human social connectivity, understanding, and access to a specific society or community was unknown to the French and they needed to recruit assistants who were able to interpret those languages. The interpreters trained "in schools of St. Louis ignored Sudanese languages".[37] The colonial forces, therefore, had a serious problem to establish their power in those territories.

Consequently, the aim of building schools at the time of French colonial oppression was to install the colonial power. According to the same source cited earlier, the opening of schools in the former French Sudan became indispensable because they felt the desire to interact with the people, the need to communicate in the local languages, at least in the early moments of the conquest, which were able to understand a little French. Ba & Taylor poignantly discussed in the Fortunes of Wangrin one of the main reasons of creating French schools in Mali. Importantly, the creation of schools originated from fear of losing citizens' favors to the advantage of local leaders.

> At the same time, the French feared that chiefs and leading citizens might offer their loyalty to Yorsam in case he should manage to establish the least military advantage over the French troops. As a guarantee against this contingency, they founded the school for Hostages in Kayes and enrolled all the children of pre-eminent families either amicably or coercion.[38]

It came to be understood that the creation of schools was not to help inculcating young boys with new knowledge, but rather it was aimed to force the parents of young Africans to collaborate with the French colonial administration in its conquest of territories and minds. In addition, the creation of such schools brought confusion in the role of the traditional society mainly based on the Malian way of doing things which became no longer relevant vis-à-vis in the French eyes. These educated young African children were considered

---

[37] Denise Bouche.(1966) Les écoles françaises au Soudan à l'époque de la conquête. 1884-1900. Cahiers d'etudes africaines. p229

[38] Ba, A. H. (1999). *The fortunes of Wangrin*. Indiana University Press. p6

superior to their own people, but nowhere close to the oppressive forces. Children had to leave their families and communities to join the French school and later to work in a distant territory for the same administration.

It was late in the nineteenth century that the creation of schools in the West African colonies began to fall into place under the authority of the French colonial administration in accordance with some religious leaders. The first school systems and the first educational policies were established. Importantly, the first school in the French Sudan was founded between 1884 and 1896 in Kayes, Kita and Bafoulabe followed by the ones of Timbuktu and Segou. It is interesting to know that on that date the French occupation was only restricted to a few military barracks from Kayes to Bamako which ensured the supply of the rivers Senegal and Niger. It was within those military barracks that the first French schools were created to educate sons of chiefs and hostages in order to become facilitators between the French colonial forces and the inhabitants of the regions.[39]

Based on the argument of different sources, it was without a doubt that the schools that the French were going to build in these territories aimed to establish their colonial power or policy. The school of the hostages *Ecole des Otages40* was built by General Joseph Gallieni in Kayes in early December 1886 and then in Kita and Bafoulabe. The argument behind the construction of those schools was to recruit by force the sons of the different local kings in order to control and train them to become French auxiliaries. Moreover, the curriculum of these schools was designed to help Africans to acquire the basics in French and mathematics.

In 1887, the majority of the military barracks were schools in the French Sudan. These schools were later removed due to financial reasons, but excluded were the school of hostages of Kayes and the

---

[39] Bâ, A. H. (1984). Amkoullel, l'enfant peul [Amkoullel The Fulani child]. France: Actes Sud.

[40] Ecole des Hotage or Hostage schools are schools created by the French colonizer in Senegal and French Sudan (Mali) where the sons of chief and notables are forcibly recruited to supervise and train them to become auxiliaries to the colonial power

Catholic mission of Kita. It was Louis Archinard, the successor of Joseph Gallieni, who engendered these changes in the 1890s in the French Sudan as Bouche explained. According to the same sources, new schools were built under the command of a new authority. Louis Edgar Trentinian, who was governor between 1895 and 1899, opened new schools to train junior auxiliaries to the French administration in the colony such as interpreters, clerks and employees of shops. They tried by educating Africans to make them docile and to suppress any attempt to résistance. The name of the "School for Hostages" was changed to the School of the Chiefs' Sons and of the Interpreters in order to achieve the colonial aspirations. These different schools were created by military commanders in the country to help them facilitate their missions. The education was indubitably male orientated based on the agenda of the colonial force on the ground. There were no women in these schools because during the same time period in Europe, the role of women in the army was null or inexistent, which means that the army and Africa was considered a dangerous ground to send women.

Moreover, African men at the early times of the French colonial oppression were concerned about the education of young boys, which attests that: "In 1888 in Kayes, they are about fifty, ten to seventeen years old, in blue Arab pants, yellow robe and small red fez."[41] Despite the intrinsic meaning of school in individual, even in community life, it did not address the need of the local people. In a word, that was not the primary objective of the French direct rule.

Since women were seen inept to fulfill those needs at that time, their education was not of any importance even though there was a need of their expertise in other domains. The history of establishing schools in the French Sudan met difficulties due to the colonial, religious and certain African values. Parents were skeptical to send their young girls to school. They feared the type of education young girls were going to receive from the colonial schools. The attitude

---

[41]   Denise Bouche.(1966) Les écoles françaises au Soudan à l'époque de la conquête. 1884-1900. Cahiers d'études africaines. p235

of the French colonial administration reinforced the philosophy of African mothers toward their daughters going to a Western school, which first kept women from school and then trained them to become good companions for African literate men. It is not a secret that a low level of literacy and education hinders African women in general and particularly Malian women's social advancement.

The lack of education and the traditional society has slowed down women's political activism in Africa, which has also played a major part in their non-presence on the political scene. Girls' parents, specifically the mother, found it was "a scandal to send a young girl to school."[42] They believed that a young girls place was near her mother in the kitchen to learn how to cook and take care of her own family like it had been going on for decades in the traditional society.

Young Girls' Education in Traditional Malian Society

In their schooling, the different types of education young girls experienced in Africa in the past contributed to shape their life in contemporary times. Education was mainly based on the role played by both girls and boys in the society. Education in the Malian society has always been seen as hands-on activities that happened at a specific time and age in a child's life. They used this model of education to teach and instill new knowledge in young children even though the nature of the topic and the educators were sometimes different. An example is that while young girls are learning from their mothers how to take care of household chores, a young boy is learning how to hunt and bring meat home for the sauce. Though there are differences about the topics, there are similarities based on the fact that both contribute to the family's welfare. Addressing the issue of similarity, both girls and boys at night sit around their grandparents listening to

---

[42] Keita, A. (1975). *La vie d'Aoua Keita racontee par elle-meme", an autobiography.* Paris: Presence Africaine. p24

the history of their family or town. This type of education has always been a part of people's lives as this passage explains:

> Education in Mali has always been connected to life and dispensed according to the circumstances that present themselves. Such a form of education inculcated good character and good health in the young members of the community. It was designed to give children sufficient knowledge of their culture, beliefs and history, thus allowing them to participate fully in their social life.[43]

It is, therefore, important to say that informal education taught individuals about their culture as well as prepared them to become responsible citizens. This type of education has always been the pillar of the Malian society and Africa in general based on topics such as hunting, smiths, fishing, healing, and history. This education could have disappeared if it was not for the work of certain writers and researchers such as Djibril Tamsir Niane, Amadou Hampate Ba, Seydou Badian Kouyate, Aoua Keita, and Adam Ba Konare. Besides the traditional education, there was a Koranic education that mainly focused on inculcating Moslem faith and its way of life in its students. Marise Conde poignantly explains in her book Segu, the beginning of Koranic schools in Mali through Timbuktu and how students from the interior cities such as Segu used to go to Timbuktu to deepen their knowledge in the Islamic faith. The same activities were going on between the rest of Mali and the Arab world through Morocco and Egypt as described by Ibn Battuta in *Journey to West Africa*. Such schools comprised different branches of knowledge and the same thing could be said about traditional schools. Informal schools in Mali represented a group that could be categorized as symbolic, cultural, scientific, technical, philosophical, metaphysical

---

[43]   Sow, A. B. (2011) *Political Leadership in the Hand of Teachers: The Type of Leadership Teacher-Politicians Displayed on the Political Scene in Mali.* VDM Verlag Publisher.

and even historical knowledge.[44] Conversely, the colonial school or modern school happened to impose them as a way to reinforce the French colonial domination of the land conquered despite the fight from the informal and Koranic education in Mali. If the first schools created to educate young African men were experiencing a fair enrollment rate, the enrollment rate was far worse when talking about young girls' recruitment. The year girls' schools opened their doors, parents, especially girls' mothers, in a way believed that school was the sole terrain reserved for men. The green belt movement activist and a Nobel Peace Prize winner Wangari Maathai spoke about the phenomenon of girls' education based on her own personal story in a documentary film by Wanuri Kahiu titled *For Our Land* in the KTN Kenya September 26, 2011.

> The way I went to school was...accidental. I was not meant to go to school. It was my eldest brother...just was wondering why my sister is not going to school. And my mother, bless her heart, she did not see any reason why I was not going to school. And she says there is no reason.[45]

In the Malian society, many young girls had not been given the opportunity to go to school as a consequence of social taboos and the fear of Western values. The colonial policy of education that disadvantaged African girls later became a fatality for most of the girls' parents, especially the mothers who could not automatically believe that young girls, as well as young boys, could have equal access to education that they believed for a long time a property of men.

---

[44] Sow, A. B. (2011) *Political Leadership in the Hand of Teachers: The Type of Leadership Teacher-Politicians Displayed on the Political Scene in Mali*. VDM Verlag Publisher.
[45] Wanuri Kahiu titled *For Our Land* KTN Kenya September 26, 2011. p22

Young Girls Education under the French Colonial Rule

Girls' education in Africa provides the overview of women's difficult participation in their respective countries' social life due to the lack of education. Based on the Islamic and cultural values of Mali, it was not easy for the young girls to join schools considered to have Western values based on alienating them by detaching them from their values. Additionally, the attitude of the young girls' parents could be supported based on the ideology behind the French direct rule policy. This French policy of direct rule was straight forward and was aimed to make African territories under French so-called colonial rule little French. This further aimed to take away from Africans (French speaking Africa) their values and way of doing things that Senghor, the former president of independent Senegal, called alienation. Some might find the refusal and resistance of young girls' parents to send them to school as a way of self-empowerment as attested in this passage of Benoist, which states:

> If the girl is under the guardianship of her parents, her family, the elders, there is little chance that they let her follow the catechism and baptism, because they know she will claim the freedom to choose her husband or at least deny the one that the custom is planning for her.

> A Christian community cannot build itself in a stable and solid way except in Christian homes.[46]

Based on the colonial historical context and Senegal being the capital of French West African countries, girls' schools for West African regions were first created in Senegal. The first structured school for girls during the French colonial presence in the French

---

[46] Benoist, J. R. (1987). Église et pouvoir colonial au Soudan français. Administrateurs et missionnaires dans la boucle du Niger (1885-1945), Paris, Karthala. p23

West Africa or (AOF) opened its doors in 1930 in Senegal for the entire region called Normal School for Teachers *Ecole Normale d'Institutrice*. It is important to understand that the objective of this education was twofold. The first main objective was to train women teachers for the French West African region. And the second objective was to educate future spouses for the educated men. Young girls' education aimed to help reinforce the French values and presence in the colonies rather than guaranteeing young women personal progress.[47]

According to certain sources, this school of the girls had no agenda for the progress of African young girls, but rather an ideological and political agenda. Certain other sources argue that the young girls' school aimed to train accomplished housewives and good mothers. In order to achieve this goal in the territories under their control in West Africa, the French administration set up a system of education. This education focused on moral education and a few pedagogy lessons considered necessary for the reinforcement of the French colonial policy. It was later that the creation of schools for girls became important in the professional training of African women after the First World War. Girls were trained to become midwives in a department of the medical school that was created in 1918 in Senegal, considered the first initiative of the French. The second initiative came in 1930 with the institutionalization of training of visiting nurses. The same source explained that the Normal School of Rufisque was considered at that time one of the best initiatives of the French colonial administration in favor of African girls' education.

Francophone women have been victims of the French educational system that labeled them as *évoluées48* or advanced. This label has been a mark of privilege in the Malian society, which separates illiterate and literate women. This same label was used

---

[47] Barthélémy, P. (2003). La formation des Africaines à l'École normale d'institutrices de l'AOF de 1938 à 1958. Edition l'E.H.E.S.S.

[48] *Evoluées* was a label used by the French during the colonial era to refer to a native African or Asian women who had "evolved" by becoming Europeanised through education or assimilation and had accepted European values and behavior

for men as well. The colonial education system aimed to assimilate African women giving them a rank that evolved alongside their male counterparts. Advanced women were women that went to French school, were well-educated, spoke and acted like the French. These women were supposed to break away from their own social values or customs.

Young girls' education did not bring much change for the reason they showed less interest in political activities. The political argument behind intellectual women's lack of interest in politics has been explained in different ways. Some attest that women have always played the political game alongside men rather than challenging it. In this context, it becomes difficult for women political leaders to demarcate themselves from the political system established by men that merely satisfies their own interest. "Those women who are elected are often those who play according to the rules of the game, rather than challenging them."[49]. A counter argument is to understand whether women feel men hold them hostage or there is a duality of role played by both parts that they supplement one another. The answer to this question becomes problematic when we refer to the argument of Jean F. O'Barr and politics. She argued that women have been missing in political science literature and research.[50] However, what is known about women is their need to join political leadership positions and have the same responsibilities and duties as men. Men see politics as their personal domain which constitutes a barrier to women's political progress and discourages them from having political ambitions. Presently, women no longer seem to see politics in the same way as men, which is instrumental to their education.

---

[49] Sweetman, C. (2000) *Women and Leadership*. Oxfam, GB. p3
[50] Jean F. O'Barr (1975). Making the Invisible Visible: African Women in Politics and Policy. African Studies Review Vol. 18, No. 3, Women in Africa (Dec., 1975), pp. 19-27. Published by: African Studies Association

Women in the Present Day

The increase in women's education contributes today to their political ambition, economic and social advancement. The presence of women on the African political scene has brought a significant change in the last two decades as a result of their education. Generally, African women have proven their contributions in several domains in their respective societies. These contributions are noticeable in their households, economies, food production systems and politics. Women's contribution in these different domains have been highly acknowledged in their respective countries, in Africa and worldwide. In a large part, this acknowledgment of African women is due to their own energetic determination to shape, express their fears and attempt to make their voices heard in the process of decision-making. As author Sweetman explained, after the democratic event and even before then, women regrouped themselves within associations at the grassroots level to form different interest groups. These women associations, like any other associations in Mali, tried to take advantage of the new political openings by seizing leadership roles. Despite the small number of women in political leadership positions in Mali, they try to influence decision makers and international organizations through their different organizations. They are also on the political scene pressing for the same opportunities their male counterparts are enjoying in politics. However, it is not by chance that the funding system of political parties in Mali, and even the rest of African countries, is instrumental to the important participation of woman in politics. In so doing, there has been an effort to try to increase the number of women on the political arena in Africa, which is sometimes encouraged by international partners. World powers understand and support that women's presence in political leadership positions will give them a chance of political, economic and social opportunities. It becomes, therefore, important to mention that women's presence in political leadership positions can guarantee the advancement of their rights. Taking that into consideration, any action that improves women's positions in their society can simultaneously support African society as a whole, as well as improve the wider development prospects.

Despite all efforts made by women in Africa, especially in Mali, they continue to face enormous hardships in politics. The increasing acknowledgment of their participation in political leadership has not translated into a meaningful access to decision-making positions, power or resources. One should say that women would have been more appreciative if their political, economic and social dynamism were channeled into generating a real form of leadership and participation.

CHAPTER III
••

WOMEN'S PARTICIPATIPATION IN POLITICS

Mali from 1946-1960

In the early years after the Second World War, the first African women started developing political interests through activism, which marks the debut of their political history, mainly in Mali. It will be an anachronism to talk about the first political regime in Mali without talking about the independence movements in Mali. It, therefore, becomes necessary to talk about Modibo Keita who was one of the key leaders of the independence movement, not only in Mali, but also in the entire African continent and the architect of women's political involvement. The independence movement from the French and the presidency of Modibo Keita in Mali were somehow intertwined due to the direct relationship between the two activities. In order to have a clear picture about Modibo Keita's regime and Malian women's political debut, it is first necessary to understand the struggle for independence in Mali alongside women activists such as Aoua Keita and Madame Sira Diop.

Independence Movements in Mali

Independence movements in Africa provide an overview of women's political debut in Africa, especially in Mali, even though it was timid. In the aftermath of the Second World War, African countries, especially those under the French colonial oppression, were given the rights to create political parties or political organizations. They created political parties such as the African Democratic Rally (RDA) and Progressive Party of Sudan (PSP) in Mali, former (French Sudan). From 18 up to 21 October 1946, after the Second World War, these two political parties became the main parties in most of the West African countries. The branch in Mali was US-RDA (African Democratic Rally African-Union). US-RDA and PSP led the country to independence on September 22nd, 1960. The Malian section of the political party US-RDA was created from the merger, in 22 October, of the Sudanese's Bloc of Mamadou Konate, the Democratic Party of Modibo Keita and a dissident wing of the PSP. Modibo became the secretary general of the new party: US-RDA.

Even though the two political parties led Mali to independence, the role played by the PSP party in the struggle for freedom raised several questions in Mali. According to certain sources, PSP being pro-colonialist was not ready for an independent Mali.[51] It turns out that the latest political party, the PSP, was also supported by the French colonial administration. As an argument in favor of the French support to the PSP, in 1946 and 1951 legislative elections, US-RDA was followed by PSP. Mamadou Konate was the only candidate from US-RDA elected as an MP in the French National Assembly. According to the same sources, The French were concerned about an eventual election of Modibo Keita in the French National Assembly.

---

[51]   Diarrah, C. O. (1986). *Le Mali de Modibo Keita*. L'Harmattan Editions. Paris

On an April 12, 1953 municipal election in Bamako, US-RDA gained the majority in the elections and PSP was behind with a large margin. There was another victory of US-RDA in the November 18, 1956 election in Bamako and Modibo Keita became the Mayor of Bamako. The success and the popularity of US-RDA in Mali were increasing when in the 1956 legislative elections; US-RDA came first in the elections in Mali. As a result, both Modibo Keita and Mamadou Konate were elected in the French parliament. Based on the popularity US-RDA was enjoying in the Malian Society, it led the country to independence on 22 September 1960 after the collapse of the Federation of Mali.

Even though Mamadou Konate and Modibo Keita were the two key leaders of US-RDA, the work done by Aoua Keita alongside these two male leaders for the struggle for independence was of great importance. Aoua Keita was the one who criticized the Senegalese who withdrew from the Federation of Mali calling them 'traitors'; and she was the first women in Mali to occupy political seats in the country after its independence.

Women Political Debut

This section is an overview of women political involvement based on the work of some women that have been the precursors of their political participation, independence, and self-determination. African women, mainly Malian women's political appearance, is imbued with their traditional society that they played and continue to play in different political roles. It is not the *ton*52 in the Bamanan Society or the *Waalde*53 in the Fulani society that will contradict this contribution of women on the political scene in Mali. Even though this role played by women is not anyway comparable to the one they play today, it is to understand that each woman has played a key part in their given societies. In Sierra Leone, Constance Cummings-John was among the first African women to develop a political interest

---

52   Ton is an association, group, club for the Bamanan people.
53   Waalde is an association, group, club for the Fulani people.

working with market women to fight for self-command and self-actualization during the colonial era. Constance Cummings-John's political interest was developed from her own experiences and her family position. In Mali, women have played a very active role in the protest movements that overcame the French colonial domination before the democratic epoch and contributed to the collapse in 1991 of Moussa Traore's dictatorial regime. As the result of their struggle, women paid a heavy price with their lives. Without women's contribution, all changes made in the legal context and behavior in the continent would be impossible. Change happened in Mali as well as elsewhere on the continent because of the assiduity and the determination of women leaders. This is to attest that women were the basis of many changes in Mali such as marriage code and guardianship, the decolonization movement, the emancipation movement, fight against excision, the birth of single political party, keeping girl mothers in school, women organization, union of French Sudanese women, Social Committee of Women Workers, Pan African Women's Organizations, and women in Mali have proved themselves through their activism. For example, women played a preponderant role in the 1946 strike organized by the Dakar-Niger railway workers. In 1947, Senegalese women organized a protest march from Thies to Dakar in support of the railroad workers, which was a testimony to female authority and resilience. The resilience of women forced the management of the railway company to negotiate on equal terms with the workers, and to accept to meet their demands.[54]

Women's participation in politics, like what is known today as the Western model, was started by women leaders for the struggle of independence and women's rights and social progress. A few key figures marked the fight for independence in Africa, among whom were Aoua Keita of Mali who graduated from the medical school of Senegal, Caroline Faye Diop of Senegal, Mrs. Jeanne Martin Cissé of Guinea and Madam Sira Diop of Mali all graduated from the Normal Teacher School of Rufisque in Senegal, Jacqueline Ki-Zerbo

---

[54] Okolo M. S. C. (2013). African Literature as Political Philosophy. Published by Zed Books Ltd

of Burkina Faso graduate of English at the Sorbonne, Jeane Gervais of Cote D'Ivoire graduated from Ecole Normal Superieure of Saint-Cloud, Henriette Dagry Diabate of Cote d'Ivoire graduate of the State Doctorate in History at the Sorbonne, were all highly educated women. Aoua was the first woman Member of Parliament in Mali who contributed to the elaboration of Malian code of marriage and guardianship which was a step forward for the rights of Malian women. She created the women inter-union movement, which she represented in 1957 at the Constituent Congress of the general union of Black African workers.

On the Malian political scene, two women, Aoua Keita and Sira Diop, happened to demarcate themselves through their hard work, sense of patriotism, and their spirit of sacrifice for their country as well as for the rest of the African continent. Even though their political activism happened at around the same time, it is to deem that both emerged at a crucial moment in the Malian, as well as the African, history. If one made a reputation at the early time of the independence, the other one emerged at the time when the wind of multi-party democracy started to blow in the continent after the fall of the Berlin Wall and the Soviet Union. The first activist cited here Aoua Keita, joined the political movements at the time when African countries needed leaders to guide them through that difficult time and usher them to independence.

Aoua Keita Political Activism

The political activism of Aoua Keita is characterized by the dualism between the power of the colonial influences and the Malian traditions. The Book *Life of Aoua Keita, narrated by her*, portrays the life of an intellectual woman that tried to fight against two forces that did not give much room to women. Under the burden of these two forces, certain African women tried to take their destiny in their own hands, and among those women were Aoua Keita, Jeanne Martin Cissé, Jacqueline Ki-Zerbo, Caroline Faye Diop, Jeanne Gervais, Jeanne Chapman, and Henriette Diabaté who were pioneers in the struggle of African women's liberation and emancipation.[55] Conversely, Aoua Keita as well as her comrades completed a brilliant education in their respective countries that led them to the African medical school or Superior School of French West Africa of Dakar in Senegal and became nurses and instructors. She worked in different regions with women in the French West African territories as a nurse, but it was her political activism that brought a tremendous change in her life. Aoua Keita discussed in her autobiography that she joined politics because of the encouragement and the support from her husband sharing with her his political passion.[56]

It was women political activists such Aoua Keita who fought to break the shackle of oppression and tried to bring women on the forefront of the social scene. Despite the diverse political difficulties, such as the timidity of Malian women at that time and the risks of her mission, Aoua refused to bow down before the social and political pressure. Aoua Keita as she explained, was sometimes ridiculed and discouraged by her political opponents, especially men in these words:

> Thank you for your educated women that we do not know what to do with them. They are still sidelined; they never wanted to participate in political activities. For ten years we have worked together and their absence has not prevented us to move forward…what you have in mind will be difficult to achieve here.[57]

The turning point in Aoua Keita's political activism started at a time of political hostilities when she was elected Member of Parliament under the French colonial administration. It is to understand at that time despite the hostilities vis-à-vis women; Aoua was permanently

---

[55] Barthelemy, P. (2010). *Africaines et diplômées à l'époque coloniale (1918-1957)* Rennes: Presses Universitaires de Rennes, (coll. Histoire), 2010, 344 p., [préface de Catherine Coquery-Vidrovitch]

[56] Keita, A. (1975). *La vie d'Aoua Keita racontee par elle-meme"*, an autobiography. Paris: Presence Africaine.

[57] Keita, A. (1975). *La vie d'Aoua Keita racontee par elle-meme"*, an autobiography. Paris: Presence Africaine. p380

informed about the political activities by her husband. In 1945, Aoua and her husband joined US RDA, the political party that led the country to independence. Despite the gerontocratic nature of the Malian society, at the time of the fight for independence, women were still not taking part in any social meetings that discussed the life of the people. Nevertheless, Aoua expressed how her husband treated her as an equal and shared information or decisions taken during political meetings. Aoua acquired a taste for politics after her marriage and which continued growing after her election at the local assembly in Mali and the increase of support she enjoyed from women's groups.[58]

The turning point in Aoua's political activism began after her divorce due to family conflict that strongly affected her life, but she did not let that affect her passion for politics. Several sources in Mali attested that it was that separation which helped Aoua to participate fully in political activities in Mali, recruiting and encouraging other women to join the political scene. She also created women organizations and was selling newspapers for her political party.[59] Nevertheless, US RDA selected Aoua to supervise the election in the region she was serving as a nurse because of her sense of responsibility and her fight for transparency. The choice of Aoua as an election supervisor was to avoid any sort of irregularity or lack of transparency that might occur during the election time. Another reason for the choice of Aoua as an election supervisor was to try to stop certain illegal practices that they thought had been going on for so long on the political scene. In addition, the political party US-RDA supposed that the French colonial administration had its own candidates that they wanted to get elected using unscrupulous methods.

The audacity of Aoua to challenge the French colonial administration was seen as a threat to their authority and the image they represented in the colonies and therefore she was labeled "the

---

[58] Jean-Marie Volet 2007. Women's perception of French colonial life in 19th century Africa: a fascinating universe challenging conventional. Retrieved 9/26/2011 from wisdomhttp://aflit.arts.uwa.edu.au/colonies 19e eng.html Troubles post- électoraux, Afrique express N° 152,11 septembre 1997

[59] Report from Jean-Marie Volet – February 2009

little negro woman" as Aoua Keita stated.[60] In addition, the role Aoua was playing for election transparency was so pivotal in her region that she became subject to different verbal harassments. Harrassments such as aggression, reproach, bullying and threat showed the degree of Aoua's engagement as a political activist that the colonial force could not deny. For many people in Mali, the hardship Aoua was experiencing on the political scene illustrated that Aoua's activism had a serious impact on her people which the colonial power could not admit. In the same vein, the French colonial administration organized the Malian political scene in way to engage a fight against Aoua based on the fact she was a woman and ready to challenge their colonial authority. During the colonial time in Africa, mainly in Mali, politics was considered the sole domain of men, and women were not supposed to venture into this unknown territory. Another argument is that if Aoua was supporting the French colonial propaganda like many other Malians did, she would have been supported by the same colonial administration, and treated as an example of a dedicated woman.

Elected to the Political Bureau of the Sudanese Union RDA in 1958, Aoua was the only woman at the time who was elected at the highest political position. In September of the same year, she was appointed after the referendum a member of the Constitutional Committee of the Republic of Sudan. It was in 1959 that her political career experience greatly changed when she was elected a Member of Parliament and continued to play a major role in politics. Aoua's political activism took a drastic change after the 1968 military coup that overthrew Modibo Keita's regime. As a dedicated politician, Aoua Keita was honored with several awards: Gold Medal of Independence of Mali, she was raised to the rank of Grand Officer of the National Order of Senegal, Merit of the Red Cross of the Empire of Ethiopia, Grand Commander of the Order of the Star of Africa and Liberia, Officer of the National Order of Dahomey current Benin.[61]

---

[60] Keita, A. (1975). *La vie d'Aoua Keita racontee par elle-meme", an autobiography*. Paris: Presence Africaine.p109

[61] Keita, A. (1975). *La vie d'Aoua Keita racontee par elle-meme", an autobiography*. Paris: Presence Africaine.

The merit an individual gains on the political scene is always related to characteristics that a leader needs to have. The distinction Aoua gained demonstrated that there was no doubt about the leadership characteristic she displayed on the political scene in Africa, especially in Mali. The risks Aoua took to fight the French oppressive colonial administration and certain Malian customs sent her to exile and reduced her to silence after the 1968 military coup. In order to achieve their goals, the method used by the French colonial administration was to make certain that the colonial administration workers engaged a fight against Aoua so that she gave up her political ambition and her fight for Mali's independence, as they confronted her in these terms "We all have received the order to...[to fight you]" stated Aoua Keita.[62] Despite those different attacks against Aoua, she did not abandon the fight for independence and the emancipation of Malian women even though the same emancipation of African women has still a long way to go, concomitantly on the social and political basis. Aoua Keita was not alone in this fight as mentioned earlier; she was joined by Mrs. Sira Diop for the progress and the emancipation of African women.

Mrs Sira Diop Political Activism

Known feminist, Mrs. Sira Diop was one of the first woman intellectuals of Mali that went to the Normal School of Rufisque in Senegal. She was also known as the first woman in Mali to get her baccalaureate degree at a time when sending young girls to French schools to pursue a career was seen as a break from the traditional society.[63] Mrs. Sira Diop was a founding member of the Inter-Sudanese women workers, and she was at the same time a founding member and president of the Union of Sudanese Women Workers (USF) that was created in 1958. Two years later, she became the chair of the constituent congress of the Women's Union of West Africa

---

[62]   Keita, A. (1975). *La vie d'Aoua Keita racontee par elle-meme", an autobiography*. Paris: Presence Africaine.p71

[63]   Bâ, A. H. (1984). Amkoullel, l'enfant peul [The Fulani child]. France: Actes Sud.

(UFOA) in Bamako. She has attested in recent years her strong support to the new family code in Mali, believing that it will help social, political and economic progress. She was appointed chair of the National Union of Malian Women (NUMW) and was awarded with the *Renaissance Africaine des Femmes d'Afrique de l'Ouest* (RAFAO) or the (African Renaissance of West African Women (ARWAW) prize on the behalf of West African women. She was a strong advocate for women emancipation. She had always been on the forefront in the struggle for the emancipation of women through different international organizations such as UNESCO and SOS children channeled toward women empowerment.

Mrs. Sira fought on different fronts in order to bring back to their senses women organizations or political leaders. The recent intervention of Mrs. Sira Diop was her 2001 mediation within a group of facilitators to persuade the former president of Niger, Mamadou Tandja, to leave power after his mandate. In 2008, she also mediated between the protagonist women's organizations in Mali *Cafo64*. Despite Mrs. Sira Diop's activism and the help she benefited from the Malian people, her support in favor of the new family code in Mali did not make unanimity among Malians. This divergence was the proof that the model of society they had fought for since the debut of the struggle for independence had a long way to go before becoming a reality. Mrs. Sira Diop's argument about the Mali family code was that:

> The code must be passed because there are options in it. We women, we fought for this code since the 50s. Since the Congress of Women in West Africa, we have participated in the elaboration of the draft code. I presented myself a document to the President of the National Assembly at the time. Mali is not an Islamic republic! I am for the adoption of this code, which will enable all communities to be under a common law (from direct conversation with Mrs. Sira DIOP).

---

[64] *Cafo* is a group of NGOs and Women's Associations in Mali that wants to contribute to promoting the status of women through training and information activities, advocacy and lobbying.

Based on the irreplaceability of women and the role they play in the society, they become indispensable in politics mainly in the democratic system, and not because they represent more than half of the world's population. Even though women have played predominant roles in the conquest of independence, mainly in Africa, the fight for their emancipation remains the primary obstacle in the continent. The different adversities women in Africa have met in the fight for their rights still remain a reality even though tremendous changes were made.

Until the 1990s, it was unheard of for an African woman to run for the presidency of her country. To be sure, Africa had a few female rulers earlier in the twentieth century, but none had been elected. Empress Zauditu, for instance, ruled Ethiopia from 1917 to 1930; Queen-regents Dzeliwe Shongwe (1982–83) and Ntombi Thwala (1983–86) reigned over Swaziland; and Elizabeth Domitien of the Central African Republic was appointed as Africa's first female prime minister, serving in 1975–76. It was only in the 1990s, however, that significant numbers of African women began aspiring to positions of national leadership.[65]

The only women involved in politics at the early times of independence in Africa were educated and were either from an intellectual family or had an intellectual husband that initiated his wife into politics. This same trend of women involvement in politics in most African countries still remains the same. Most of those women have European values which is the cause of divergence between them and the mass of illiterate women they are supposed to represent. However, their political opening, that made an impact in the African political arena in the 1990s, contributed to emancipate women on the political scene, deserves to be valued. However other graduates from the Normal Teacher School of Rufisque in Senegal happened to play important roles in the political life of their country. Caroline Faye Diop of Senegal was among the first great unionist in her country.

---

[65] Tripp, A. M. (2001). Women and Democracy: THE NEW POLITICAL ACTIVISM IN AFRICA. Journal of Democracy Volume 12, Number 3 July 2001.p141

Caroline Faye Diop Political Activism

A fervent activist and feminist, Caroline Faye Diop was among the women's groups that created the women branch of the Senegalese Progressive Union '*Union Progressiste Senegalais*'. She was for the first time in the history of Senegalese to become in 1963 the first elected member of the parliament. Once in office, Caroline Faye Diop started addressing the needs of women to make a living and the creation of a family code in Senegalese that would protect the rights of women. And she was the only woman to participate in the vote for the family code, being the sole woman member of parliament. Caroline Faye Diop played an important leadership position in the National Assembly and was elected in 1964 the chairperson of the Senegalese Progressive Union of Women. Caroline Faye Diop was the women minister in Senegal and Vice Deputy Secretary of the Pan- African women. She occupied different ministerial positions; and was first appointed Minister of Social Action in 1978, Minister Delegate to the Prime Minister in 1981 and then Minister of State in 1982. While she was in the ministerial office, she created different interest groups for the promotion of Senegalese women. She has been a strong advocate of women's rights and she even happened to protest before President Senghor as to why women remain quiet during the Congress of the party, and not a single woman happens to say a word.

Caroline Faye Diop remained the only women in the National Assembly for a decade in Senegal before other women could be elected to that position. Conversely, she had to fight adversity on the political scene, especially, from her counterpart men for she was seen as a threat for being able to mobilize other women and make a place in politics. For Babacar and Waly Diaye, Caroline Faye Diop's main fight in politics was against men in her own political party that did not want to see a woman enjoying the same privilege and becoming successful. Like many women politicians in Africa, Caroline Faye Diop was married to an influential politician from her country who was assassinated during his time in office.[66] She was the author of different actions such as the promotion and the improvement of women conditions in Senegal. Caroline Faye Diop has always considered herself a feminist, but especially a feminist who fights for equality between men and women. If she was fighting alongside her husband on the political scene, Jacqueline Marie Therese Ki Zerbo kept a low profile hidden behind her husband on the political scene.

Jacqueline Marie Therese Ki Zerbo Political Activism

A Sorbonne graduate, Jacqueline Ki Zerbo was an English teacher in Burkina Faso before asserting her skills in international institutions. She was a mother figure to her students more than a teacher. Jacqueline Ki Zerbo's education and great knowledge of different subjects allowed her to occupy different administrative positions in her country. For a long time, she remained a director of the Normal School for young girls. A founding member of the Female Voltaic Assistance and an advocate for fervent social activities, Jacqueline Ki Zerbo has always fought for women emancipation. She was among the key protestors in January 3, 1966 that required the departure of Maurice Yameogo from power who finally resigned under street pressure. For a few years, she has been in charge of a union press in Burkina Faso, the voice of the teacher. Jacqueline Ki Zerbo's work ethic and dedication to development programs and young girls' education helped her achieve international recognition, nominations and the Paul G. Hoffman prize in 1984. Despite her activism, Jacqueline Ki Zerbo always remained beside her husband on the political scene.

In order to understand the progress made by women in politics, it is important to revisit the different republics that succeeded in power in Mali. Even though the experience of women in political leadership is not always encouraging, women still continue to occupy the leadership position in the continent.

---

[66] Babacar Ndiaye. B; Ndiaye. W (2006). *Présidents et ministres de la République du Sénégal*, Dakar, Senegal.

CHAPTER IV

••

THE DIFFERENT REPUBLICS OF MALI

Since its declaration of independence from the French in 1960 up to the year 2012, Mali has experienced five (5) political regimes and one (1) interim government. There were two military coups and three democratically elected presidents and none of them was a woman. Women's presence was not significant under the first two republics. They started joining the political scene in mass after the 1991 democratic event in Mali and elsewhere in Africa. Surprisingly, the different military coups did not affect women's political participation in Mali; they did, however, contribute to an increase in women participation in politics. And the Modibo Keita regime or the first republic opened political activities to women in Mali.

Modibo Keita and
the First Republic of Mali 1960-1968

The first republic of Mali symbolizes not only the early times of African experience of self-governance, decision making and the first experience of women in politics, but also how they join the political scene. African women were seriously handicapped by their lack of education when Mali acquired its independence in the end of 1960. The French colonial education system, that was in place before the country gained its sovereignty, was not designed to serve the needs of the independent French West African territories in general and in particular independent Mali. The literacy rate at independence was at a very low-level and only a small number of the African population attended school, while a large number of the population was illiterate, mainly women. Despite women's emancipation, they never played real political roles under the French colonial rule. They were at the same time disadvantaged on the educational, political and economic basis.[67] The disadvantage of Malian women was instrumental to the colonial policy continued after the proclamation of its independence.

Mali became independent after Senegal withdrew from the Federation of Mali which comprised (Senegal and French Sudan) and took the name Mali. The country conferred upon itself different priorities on the national as well as on the international level and expressed its choice for a socialist system which could be argued at its time. This political choice based on a socialist economy did not happen without making political enemies. After the independence of Mali, Modibo Keita the first democratically elected president, was involved in a different movement of independence and affirmed his firm solidarity to all African countries. He proposed to the rest of African leaders the creation of a single currency and a market that could face foreign markets. However, after US- RDA's control of the political scene in Mali, it became the only political party in the country based on the centralism democratic system. The single party led the

---

[67] Diarrah, C. O. (1986). *Le Mali de Modibo Keita*. L'Harmattan Editions. Paris.

National Political Bureau (NPB) and several members of this same bureau were in the government. The President Modibo Keita became Secretary General of the US-RDA. The Minister of Planning and Rural Economy, Seydou Badian Kouyaté, was Secretary of Economic, Social and Cultural Affairs. The Minister of Interior, Mamadou Keita Madaïra, was Secretary to the Administrative and Judicial Affairs. The Minister of Public Service, Labor and Social Affairs, Ousmane Ba, was Press Secretary. The Minister of Information, Mamadou Gologo, was Conflict Commissioner. The Minister of State, Jean-Marie Koné, was Secretary for External Relations. The Deputy Foreign Minister, Baréma Bocoum, was Member of the Foreign Affairs Commissions.

Even though there were no women in the government, two women were at the national parliament, Aoua Keita and Mrs. Touré Kamissa Diallo, and one city councilor, Mrs. Aminata Diop. Malian women, before independence, have played a significant role in the fight against the French colonial oppressive forces and the feudal authority. This fight was mostly led by illiterate women at that time. They nonetheless played the part of the mobilizers and facilitators of the main political parties at the time. It, therefore, becomes difficult to talk about politics in Mali without mentioning the role played by women at all levels in the society that ushered Mali to independence. Among the women that played preponderant roles was Aoua Keita, a key leader of Malian women that were engaged in the struggle for independence, and Mrs Sira Diop.

There was no woman among the members of the national political bureau that had a ministerial seat. However, there was a strong division within the national political bureau and despite the different interventions of President Modibo Keita to solve the issues; he ended up dissolving the National Political Bureau. It was in 1968 after the dissolution of the National Political Bureau that he was overthrown by a military coup led by Colonel Moussa Traore, whose regime was not at first open to women.

Moussa Traore and the Second Republic 1968-1991

The years 1968 to 1991 marks the first time real political leadership for women came into being, which continues to improve in Mali. In 1968, Lieutenant Moussa Traore, the head of the Military Committee of National Liberation (MCNL)[68] with his companions Captain Yoro Diakite, Captain Charles Samba Cissoko, Captain Mamadou Sissoko, Lieutenant Moussa Traore, Lieutenant Youssouf Traore, Lieutenant Tiékoro Bagayogo, Lieutenant Filifing Sissoko, Lieutenant Karim Dembele, Lieutenant Missa Kone, Lieutenant Mamadou Sanogo, Lieutenant Kissima Doukara, Lieutenant Baba Diarra, Lieutenant Mara and Captain Joseph Malick Diallo overthrew Modibo Keita's socialist regime and dissolved the single party US-RDA. There were no women involved in the coup and they did not take part or occupy leadership positions in the first transitional government. The leaders of US-RDA were imprisoned and the party loyalists continued its activities underground. Captain Yoro Diakite became the head of a transitional government, the constitution was suspended and the political parties banned from all activities. According to different sources, the November 19, 1968 coup was encouraged by the dissolution of both the national assembly and the political party, adoption of the socialist system and the lack of democratic organizations. Once in power, the MCNL banned all political activities and led the country with an iron fist. It established a police state under the leadership of one of the coup leaders, Colonel Tiécoro Bagayoko. Schools were quickly targeted as the number one enemy of the military regime because of their loyalty to the former president. In order to subdue the threat of the action of teachers, the MCNL sent intelligence officers to visit schools and investigate the curriculum of the professors. Three days after the military coup, a transitional government was formed with fourteen ministers, of which there were no women.

---

[68] MCNL, the Military Committee of National Liberation was a Malian military junta that came to power by coup d'etat in November 1968.

- Captain Yoro Diakite (President of the Transitional Government),
- Jean-Marie Koné (Minister of State for Foreign Affairs and Cooperation),
- Louis Negro (Minister of Finance, Planning and Economic Affairs),
- Mamadou Aw (Minister for Industry and Infrastructure),
- Dr. Henry Corenthin (Minister of Transport, Public Works and Telecommunications),
- Captain Charles Samba Cissoko (Minister of National Defense),
- Squadron Leader Kone Balla (Information Minister, in charge of Security)
- Ibrahima Sall (Minister of Justice),
- Bénitiéni Fofana (Minister of Health),
- Zanga Coulibaly (Minister of Production),
- Boubacar Diallo (Minister of Public Service and Labour),
- Yaya Bagayogo (Minister of National Education, Youth and Sports),
- Mrs. Cissé, Inna Sissoko (State Secretary for Social Affairs),
- Konate Tiéoulé (CEO of the Development Bank of Mali with ministerial rank).

They reshuffled the transitional government six days later with the creation of a new ministry and one minister allocated to a woman, Mrs. Cissé Inna Sissoko. Cissé Inna Sissoko. A former social worker, Mrs. Cissé Inna Sissoko was the first woman to become a member of a government in Mali. On December 7, 1968, a new Ministry was created, the Ministry for the Presidency of the Transitional Government, led by Hamaciré N'Douré.

Surprisingly, there were only two members of the CMLN in the transitional government. The military planned to tackle the economic recovery and withdrew quietly to their barracks at the end of this mission. As political experts have stated "Power corrupts and absolute power corrupts absolutely." Not only did the military fail to keep their promise, but they also continued to give mixed messages to the people. If at first the military government assigned itself the mission to take care of the economic recovery before returning to the barracks, they went back saying that as soon as the conditions of a genuine democracy were met, they would leave power. Even though the CMLN made the solemn declaration to ensure the people about their oath to return to their camps once the conditions were met, they ended by confiscating the power. This is tangible proof that the time the military spent in the leadership position helped them to acquire a taste for political leadership. They confiscated power, freedom of liberty and remained in power for decades. The military continued to oppress intellectuals and maintained the single party system until its fall.

In 1969, they reshuffled the transitional government and the head of the government left the presidency for a ministerial cabinet. The leader of the CMLN, Moussa Traore became the head of the new government. Another reshuffle in the government took place in 1974 after the arrest of his coup partners and a new constitution was adopted by referendum and new ministerial positions allocated to a woman. Importantly in the history of Mali, women were on the road to political leadership facilitated by the government of the Second Republic. Mrs. Cissé Inna Sissoko was the first woman Minister in Mali followed by Mrs. Gakou Fatou Niang, Mrs. Sidibé, Astan Cissé, and Mrs. Diallo, Lalla Sy.

- 1969-74 Secretary of State for Social Affairs, Marian Inna Sissoko Cisse
- 1980-85 Minister of Information and Telecommunication, Mrs. Gakou, Fatou Niang
- 1986-88 Minister of Social Affairs and Health, Mrs. Sidibe, Aissata Cisse

It is interesting to know that even though these political leadership positions were not considered fundamental in the government, men were for the first time forced to compromise with women regarding the political leadership positions. The increase of the number of women will later be linked to an international event that brings women on the forefront of the political scene in Africa and mainly in Mali.

The referendum adopted the creation of a single party, the election of a president democratically elected and the creation of a national assembly after the end of the transitional government scheduled for five years. In 1976, the government of Mali created a single party, Democratic Union of the People of Mali (UDPM), along with different other unions to reinforce the power of the single party: Labor Union of Mali, National Union of the Youth of Mali, National Union of Women of Mali, National Union of Pupils and students of Mali. These organizations had representation in the national assembly and in government.

In 1979's presidential and legislative elections, Moussa Traore, the single candidate at the presidential election, was elected with eighty-two (82) members of the national assembly. It is to say that the creation of the single party UDPM became an important turning point in Malian women's political leadership. Ministry of Information was the first cabinet allocated to a woman in government in 1982. A few years later more women joined Moussa Traore's government. In 1988, a second woman joined the government and was appointed Minister of Health followed by a third woman who remained in government until the 1991 coup that overthrew Moussa Traore's regime.

- 1980-85 Minister of Information and Telecommunication, Mrs. Gakou Fatou Niang

- 1986-88 Minister of Social Affairs and Health, Mrs. Sidibe, Aissata Cisse

- 1988-91 Minister of Employment and the Civil Services, Mrs, Diallo, Lalla Sy

Mrs. Diallo, Lalla Sy, who was appointed Minister of Labor in 1988, was also the last woman to have an important leadership position during Moussa Traore's presidency as claimed by many Malians. It was during the leadership of Mrs. Diallo, Lalla Sy as the Labor Minister that an international event or structural adjustment pushed by the institutions of the Bretton Woods was implemented in Mali. The application of structural adjustment had brought an important number of victims due to the liquidation, justification and privatization of the state firms. The only woman Minister, Mrs. Diallo at the time, had to face the complex problem such as the difficulty of providing jobs to the people. In a sense, Mrs. Diallo being the Minister of Labour, the question of how to find a solution rested on her shoulders.

In addition to the ministerial positions, they appointed a woman Deputy Secretary General during Moussa Traore's regime which could be considered at that time a very important political cabinet position where the position of prime minister was non-existent. Several researchers pointed out women politicians' contribution to the establishment and reinforcement of Moussa Traore's single party in Mali. In addition, women have played important roles through the National Union of Women of Mali (called UNFM in French), which was a political branch that grouped all women in the country. Women had been active in the Labor Union of Mali, National Union of the Youth of Mali, and National Union of Pupils and students of Mali. Additionally, women continued to play important roles on the political scene until the wind of democracy started blowing toward Africa, which started in Eastern Europe, reached Mali and put an end to the dictatorial regime of Moussa Traore and ushered the country to a multi-party democracy.

Importantly, the educated women that fought against the military regime had a clear vision for their respective countries and Africa in general. Malian women regrouped under political organizations for instance UNFM/NUMW Union National des Femmes du Mali (Malian Women National Union) engaged a pitiless struggle for democracy against Moussa Traore's dictatorial regime. Several women paid a capital price for the advent of democracy in their country.

The first democratic organizations in the country were created in 1990: the National Congress of Democratic Initiative (CNID) and the Alliance for Democracy in Mali (ADEMA), the Pupils and Students Association, the Malian Association of Human Rights

(AMDH) joined by the Labor Union to force Moussa Traore to adopt a multi-party democracy. The protests of democratic organizations were severely oppressed and several people killed which led to the coup d'etat led by General Amadou Toumani Toure. Here again, women played important roles in the people's uprising movement for democracy. The participation of women was through democratic organization and newspapers, as well as the transitional government that elected a Democratic president. People such as Mrs. Diakite Sanaba Sissoko, Mrs. Traoré Salimata Tamboura, Mbam Diarra (AMDH), Many Camara, and Mrs. Sy Kadiatou Sow fought for a new political system in the country (Thiam, Bamanet August 31, 2012). The fight for a multiparty democratic system facilitated women's political integration and allowed women to address their agenda.

Women and the Transitional Government 1991-1992

The transitional government in Mali provides ample detail about the creation of political parties in Mali, and the contribution of women leaders on the political scene as well as the role they played in the transitional government. Lieutenant Colonel Amadou Toumani Toure, known as ATT, led a coup organized by the Transition Committee for the Salvation of the People (CTSP) that overthrew Moussa Traore's regime. At first Toure was very popular for being the savior of the people from the military oppression. He promised and kept his promise to return back to the military barracks at the end of the transitional period. The transitional government CTSP presided from 1991-1992. It organized the trial of the members of Moussa Traore's regime, organized the transition and a multi-party democratic election. During this period, several political parties emerged and women played significant roles in the transitional government. In Mali, women for the first time were governors and ambassadors, and controlled certain strategic ministerial positions in the country. Women became Secretary of State for the Promotion of Women, Minister of Rural Development, Department of Health and Social Affairs, and women enjoyed important political freedom. Women continued to occupy more strategic political positions after the election of the President of the Third Republic in Mali.

Among women who became popular for the fight against Moussa Traore's dictatorial regime was Mme Sy, Rokiatou Sow. A group of women that joined their forces with men as a resistance to the single party system within political associations and local organizations, organized this fight. Two democratic associations CNID and ADEMA emerged one after another as movements of resistance to Moussa Traore's single party system, and they gave the opportunity for Malians to enjoy their political activism. These two democratic associations were reinforced in their struggle for democracy, not only by AEEM a student association and workers union, but also the majority of the Malian population due to the lack of economic opportunities and the hardships of life. In general, the determination of the cited organizations and unions led Mali to the multi-party democracy. The two associations CNID and ADEMA became political parties right after the collapse of the single party regime and took concomitantly the name of CNID-*Faso Yiriwa Ton* and ADEMA-PASJ (African Party for Solidarity and Justice).

At the creation of the first democratic movement in Mali, CNID, there were only five men (Mountaga Tall, Tiémoko Garan Kouyaté, Hamidou Diabaté, Drissa Diakité and Oumar Mariko) and there were no women, according to several sources, which was contested by certain politicians. And unlike CNID, the initiators of ADEMA were both men and women that joined forces together for a common cause. The debut of the multi-party democratic regime marked the proliferation of political parties (14 parties) in Mali. In addition to the first two political parties several others made their appearance on the political scene. Among the new political parties that followed the creation of the first two political parties in addition to the two oldest political parties US-RDA and PSP, that led Mali to independence, surfaced on the political scene. Military Committee CTSP along with political parties, civil society and non-governmental organizations organized the trial for the fallen regime and the multi-party democratic election which led to the victory of Alpha Oumar Konare the candidate of ADEMA-PASJ. This new government despite women's massive involvement in regime change in Mali did not entrust many ministerial positions to women.

- 1991-92 Minister of the Environment and Rural Development Sy Maimouma Ba

- 1991-92 Minister of Health, Social Affairs and Women Sy Oumou Louise Sidebé.

- 1991-92 Minister of Planning and International Cooperation Cissé Mariam Kaïdama Sidibé.

Among the women that joined the early government of the Third Republic of Mali, there was only one of them who was well-known on the political scene in the country, the only one who openly fought for democracy in the country. It is also important to point out that Mrs. Sy's husband's family was strongly involved in politics, which could explain her political activism in the country as well as many other women. As is commonly discussed about women's political participation in the continent, family ties have been pivotal to the leadership of many women that have remained in political leadership positions for a long time and have occupied different leadership positions.

Alpha Oumar Konare and the Third Republic 1992-2002

The two-term presidency of Alpha O. Konare, or the third republic, depicts the different leadership roles played by women and the significance of those roles on the political scene. A professor of history and a former Sports and Culture Minister of General Moussa Traore's regime, Alpha Oumar Konare became in 1992 the first democratically elected president of the third republic at a free and fair election with some irregularities as noticed by the international election observers.

Konare was the candidate of Alliance for Democracy in Mali-African Party for Solidarity and Justice (ADEMA-PASJ), which became the greatest political party in Mali and served two terms in office. Several political parties participated in this election and within each political party, there was a strong representation of women. Ironically, there were no women candidates at the legislative election. It was clear that certain social reasons justified this meager representation of women such as young girls' school enrollment by Moussa Traore's political regime. In fact, what is known about young girls' education is that until the 26 March coup the number of girls enrolled was not significant, which changed under the third republic. Like the first republic, education became the main priority of the third republic, which helped in its effort by women's non-governmental organizations (NGOs) to recruit more women.

Even though Alpha Oumar Konare's election was highly contested in Mali, political parties happened to accept the result related to their past experience of democratic struggles. ADEMA- PASJ won a majority of seats in the national assembly, 76 of the 116 parliamentary seats and with 214 of the 751 seats counselors that led certain political parties to protest against the total control of the majority party over the rest of the political parties in the country. Right after the election of Alpha Oumar Konare as the first president of democratic Mali, the citizens revived with strikes. The unusual unrest did not help the work of the new government of Younnouss Toure.

Younouss Toure led the first democratic government under Alpha O. Konare's presidency in 1992 which lasted only one year due to the culmination of pressures of post electoral crises. Toure had to face several protests led by the opposition political parties, union groups, and the students' associations. This first democratic government in Mali after military reign experienced serious instabilities. It had to fight against the Democratic leaders that fought for the reintegration of multi-party democratic system, the civil society, workers' and students' unions. The Democratic leaders, except those in power, thought that their victory was taken away. Toure's government that was mainly composed of men (19 ministers) with only two women ministers could not survive the social upheaval.

In the political arena, people were expecting to have more women in ministerial positions, but that did not happen despite the encouragement of international donors to support the political parties that had more women. The two ministerial positions allocated to women were not considered key positions in the government. The excuse in this case could be that it was the debut of democratic experience in Mali after the first coup in 1968 that toppled a democratic regime. This occasion has also been looked at as a chance for anyone regardless of sex, race or social status to become a political leader in Mali, and women could not make an exception in this case. Women's presence in political leadership positions were highly supported in the political milieu despite their small number. Women see in this action a sign of encouragement and hope.

In April 1993, the culmination of pressures from the students union, opposition parties and a part of the civil society led to the departure of Youssoussi Toure's government and was replaced by Abdoulaye Sekou Sow as prime minister. This new government thought about integrating the main opposition parties at the time in the government, especially the National Congress of Democratic Initiative (CNID) by granting it some ministerial portfolios. Despite all attempts of integration of the opposition political parties in the share of power by the majority political party for its survival, this government was short-lived.

The instabilities engendered by the pressures of political parties and different unions in the country continued to mount after the nomination of Abdoulaye Sekou Sow as the new prime minister under Alpha Oumar Kanare presidency. Unlike Younoussi Toure, Sekou Sow's government went further by appointing more women to ministerial positions. Under Sekou Sow's leadership, there were four women ministers. Facing intensive social unrest in Mali, the president Alpha O. Konare changed the government for a third time in search of a solution to the problem.

The appointment of a third Prime Minister Ibrahim Boubacar Keita of the third republic was to put an end to the different protests throughout the country in which he was successful. After being appointed as Prime Minister, Ibrahim Boubacar Keita became the secretary-general of the ADEMA-PASJ, which led to the division of the major political party. The split of ADEMA-PASJ affected the rest of the political parties like an epidemic, and most of the major political parties experienced several divisions from 1990-2000. These partitions played an important role in the increase of the number of political parties in Mali as a result of the political situation in the country. As a solution to the social unrest, Ibrahim B. Keita later arrested most of the opposition leaders due to an incident that led to the killing of an undercover police officer who was off duty, according to certain sources in Mali. Among the politicians jailed, there was a woman Fanta Diarra. She was the first vice president and women's chairperson of the National Congress of Democratic Initiative CNID (Afrique Express N° 152). The tension between the government and the opposition political parties led the second to withdraw themselves from the 1997 presidential election. Despite the withdrawal of the opposition political parties from the presidential election, the president Alpha Oumar Konare kept the calendar of the presidential election in which there were only two candidates in the race Mamadou Batrou Diaby of the Party for Unity, Democracy and Progress (PUDP), a very small political party, and Alpha Oumar Konare. According to the same source cited earlier, in order to legitimize the election, he had to make a compromise with his opponent Mamadou Batrou Diaby.

In addition, the increase of political parties in the 1997 elections made the number of political parties reach twenty. As result, no political party at that time had a majority of voice to win the election and had to begin forming alliances. The former major political party ADEMA-PASJ formed an alliance with sister political parties under the National Convergence for Democracy and Progress and the opposition grouped formed the Collective of 'Political' Opposition Parties called (COPPO) in French. The irony here was that these political alliances did not last for more than a few months after the 1997 elections. The COPPO alliance aimed to defeat ADEMA-PASJ that had gripped the political apparatus of Mali which had led the opposition to boycott the 1997 elections. And because of the lack of a viable opposition candidate in the 1997 election, the candidate of ADEMA-PASJ won the presidential election.

Based on the confused situation of the 1997 election, the second term of Alpha O. Konare presidency continued to bring more discontent and divisions on the political and social scene. And more divisions happened within the ADEMA-PASJ major political party caused by the choice of a presidential candidate in the 2002 election. Importantly, women militants of the ADEMA-PASJ tried to join their forces together in the selection of a viable candidate for the presidential election. The previous coalition, which was formed in the 1997 election, left room for a new coalition composed of former political competitors to support the candidacy of an independent candidate Amadou Toumani Toure in order to block the route to the candidate of ADEMA-PASJ, and even more, to sanction this political party. Furthermore, the discomfort created within the major political party, led the former Prime Minister of ADEMA-PASJ Ibrahim Boubacar Keita to resign from the party and form his own political party which continued to weaken the majority political party. In the 2002 presidential election, the independent candidate Amadou Toumani Toure won the election and ADEMA-PASJ became the opposition political party. The position assumed by ADEMA-PASJ as the main opposition political party in Mali did not last for it later joined the new government leaving the political scene without a serious opposition that could bring a check and balance back into the democratic political system in Mali.

During the two-term presidency of Alpha Oumar Konare (10 years), there were four prime ministers and none of them was a woman even though they played important roles in the political party ADEMA-PASJ. Unlike the Prime Minister's position there were few women that served in the four governments under Konare's presidency during the Alpha Oumar Konare's two-terms in office. It is important to draw the readers' attention to the fact that most of the women politicians that served as ministers were from the political party of the president. The first government under Konare led by Prime Minister Younoussi Toure served from 1992 to 1993. This first government was made up of nineteen (19) ministers, and only two of the ministries were under women's leadership.

- 1992-1993 Fatou Haidara Minister of Labor and professional training
- 1992-93 Fatoumata Camara State Secretary to the Minister of National Education, in charge of basic education.

These Ministerial seats used by the two women Ministers in Mali were not considered key Ministerial cabinet positions in the decision-making or strategic positions in the government, which women continued to have for a long time. Simarlarly, a woman Fatou Haidara remained in the government for a long time and several people in the country continue to wonder why she was still in the government based on the fact she did not take part or was not known during the fight for multiparty democratic system events in the country. In addition, the small representation of women in President Konare's government was also explained by the unstable political and social scene.

A few months later after his appointment, Prime Minister Younoussi Toure resigned due to different tensions caused by the post-democratic election. The cohabitation between political parties became so intense in one way and in another way the struggle within the major political party in power was not enviable. In addition to those two situations cited earlier, the social and economic discontent did not help to bring peace in the country. The position of Prime Mister experienced several reshufflings based on the internal dispute within the party in government and the social unrest that remained unsolved.

After the resignation of the Prime Minister Younoussi Toure, Abdoulaye Sekou Sow was appointed as Prime Minister to manage the difficult political, economic and social unrest in the country. This time was like a test for the Malian new democracy which was born in serious agony. Sow's government was composed of nineteen ministers, including two women, also members of the major political party. The drop in the number of woman in the government at the time could be explained by the absence of opposition political parties in the government and the fight within the major political party. There were women in Sow's government who made a reputation during the fight for democracy in the country and had good relations on the Malian political scene.

- 1993-94 Minister of Foreign Affairs, Malians living abroad and of the African integration, Mme Sy Kadiatou Sow

- 1993-94 Minister of Handicraft and Tourism, Mme Fatou Haidara.

If Mme Sow was a strong militant of the major political party that fought against Moussa Traore's dictatorial regime, Mme Haidara was not known on the political scene in Mali. However, they were only the two women in the government to hold ministerial positions. It was like history repeating itself, Sow's government could survive the difficult hardship Toure's government faced. Prime Minister Abdoulaye Sekou Sow's government was composed of 19 ministers and he remained in office from 1993 to 1994 and was forced to resign and was replaced by the secretary general of ADEMA-PASJ. Prime Minister Sow discussed his resignation as instrumental to the conspiracy within his own political party against his power.[69] The ministerial positions held by women in this government were not considered significant and strategic even though some thought they were important in the role of decision-making.

The departure of Prime Minister Sow from the government opened the door to a new Prime Minister Ibrahim Boubacar Keita who was considered as the only one who could find a solution to the difficulties Malian schools were experiencing, the political struggle, and the social and economic unrest. Among the seventeen ministers that served in the government of Prime Minister Keita, there were only two ministries led by women and the number did not change.

- 1994-9 Ministry of Handicrafts, Tourism and Industry, Mrs. Fatou Haidara

- 1994-97 Minister of Urban Development and Housing, Mrs. Sy, Kadiatou Sow.

---

[69] Chahana TAKIOU (2008). Revelations of Abdoulaye Sékou Sow (II): "How late Prof. Mohamed Lamine Traoré forced me to resigned" (Les révélations de Me Abdoulaye Sékou Sow (II): «Comment feu le Pr Mohamed Lamine Traoré m'a contraint à la démission). L'INDEPENDANT – Date: 08 Septembre 2008

The representation of women continued to experience the same trend until the end of President Konare's first mandate then they experienced a considerable increase in the number in the government. However, there was a small reshuffling of the government in 1996, but that did not affect or benefit women. During the same year, a woman M. Hamaciré N'Douré became the leader of an opposition party Bloc for Democratic and Integration of Africa called (BDIA). More involvement of women took place a few months later and they started joining the political scene having access to certain strategic positions in the government. There were six ministries allocated to women out of sixteen ministries, which was a precursor in the history of governments in Mali.

- 1997-00 Minister of Industry, Trade and Handicrafts, Fatou Haidara,

- 1997-00 The Minister of Urbanism and Habitat, Mrs. Sy, Kadiatou Sow,

- 1997-00 The Minister of Health of Elderly People and Solidarity, Mrs. Diakite, Fatoumata Ndiaye.

- 1997-00 The Minister of Culture and Tourism, Aminata Dramane Traoré

- 1997-00 The Minister for the Promotion of Women, Children and Families, Mrs. Diarra, Hafsatou Thiero.

- 1997-00 The Minister of Communication, Mrs. Ascofaré, Ouleymatou Tamboura.

It is important to point out that among these ministers only two demarcated themselves with their sense of political activism. Even though there is a flagrant difference between the two ministers how they made their debut in politics and the connectivity within the society as political activists, they both played an important role in the restoration of the multiparty democratic system in Mali. Mrs. Sy, Kadiatou Sow served several times as Minister in the country and in the different governments of President Alpha Oumar Konaré. She is considered today as an emblematic figure of the democratic movement in Mali that led the toppling down of Moussa Traore military's dictatorial regime. Mrs. Sy, Kadiatou Sow also served as governor of the district of Bamako, a key political position in Mali. It is also significant to point out that Mrs Sy, Kadiatou Sow has enjoyed the following position due to the role played by her husband and in-laws that have been very influential on the country's political scene.[70] Conversely, Aminata D. Traore did not benefit from the same advantages as Mrs. Sy, Kadiatou Sow enjoyed in politics in Mali. Nevertheless, she is a confirmed woman activist in Mali even in Africa and played some international roles, which allowed her to make a way into politics. Aminata D. Traore is today the equivalent of *Nyeleni* in Mali who is a Bamanan figure of a brave woman. She demarcated herself by going further in her political activism becoming alter-globalist in the defense of developing countries and opposing the attitudes and the dictate of the world powers as she testifies in this passage.

> Ignorance, I'm talking about and which seems more serious than poverty, is true in a strategic area as the state of mineral wealth, that we draw and how that money is managed. Those who, from the outside, pour crocodile tears for the poor in Africa should allow first Africans, namely the poor, to understand how the continent's vast natural resources contribute to the prosperity of multinational and local contacts. There is much to say also about agricultural materials. The government and bureaucrats have benefited more than the peasants of the time when these raw materials – cotton, peanuts, coffee, cocoa, – were better paid. What are the benefits of growth to be for the people? Very little. Infrastructure? We must look closely at the mechanisms for financing projects and findings to understand the extent to which donors and client countries and good students are away from

---

[70]   Barthelemy, P. (2010). *Africaines et diplômées à l'époque coloniale (1918-1957)* Rennes: Presses Universitaires de Rennes, (coll. Histoire), 2010, 344 p., [préface de Catherine Coquery-Vidrovitch]

people. They do not benefit more from the little that is done. The power lines overlooking the villages and slums where live "poor" to go enlighten those who can afford to pay their electricity bill.[71]

Aminata D. Traore poignantly argued against the excesses of democracy and the attitudes of politicians. She believes that the Malian citizens are left out in the share of the national resources. Even though her fight brought controversy in the world, including Mali, it is to acknowledge that she is acclaimed in the developing world and considered a hero. Aminata D. Traore, a sociologist, made her political debut in Cote d'Ivoire working under the Minister of Women of Cote d'Ivoire, she then worked for a UNDP (PROWWESS / Africa) regional project to promote the role of women and disadvantaged communities in the management of water and sanitation. It was through this position that Aminata D. Traore has made a name on the international scene. She served as Minister of Culture and Tourism of Mali from 1997 to 2000. Aminata Traoré's involvement on the ground in local actions is to provide opportunities and visions that can bring at the same time a bright future for Mali and Africa.

Aminata D. Traore has proven herself in many domains in the society, such as her neighborhood grassroots action. She was the first person to encourage communities in Bamako to begin paving their streets to keep the city clean and to contribute to the development of the city. The paving project continued and gained funding from the Luxembourg Cooperation based on the success realized by Aminata D. Traore in her neighborhood Missira. Under the leadership of Aminata D. Traore, the neighborhood planted hundreds of trees and set up small-scale infrastructure for women and children. Despite the tremendous role played by people in the neighborhood, they faced difficulties at the local administration level as she states here, quoted by Yattara and Perrin:

---

[71] Aminata Dramane Traoré. Une révoltée altermondialiste 21 mai 2008, Bamako (Mali). Propos recueillis par Sadou Yattara et Anne Perrin retieved 4/15/13 http://www.oecd.org/fr/csao/publications/41682765.pdf. p5

Now I know from experience that the enormous difficulty of acting on the field with populations resulting from conflicts of legitimacy. The elected officials do not necessarily want to have to deal with organized civil society, informed and dynamic. Moreover, everything is in French, a language that the vast majority of the population does not speak or understand.[72]

Aminata Drame continued her grass-root actions and activism despite the rivalries from the political parties as she discussed in her statement. The time she spent in Ibrahim Boubacar Keita's government helped her to better understand the political scene. Inversely, Prime Minister Keita led the country with an iron fist oppressing the opposition political parties and the student's union. Certain sources in Mali portrayed Keita as the man who kept the peace in Mali and avoided Alpha Oumar's regime to collapse. It was also under Keita's government that women had a strong representation in the government despite the reduction of ministerial positions.

According to certain sources, it was instrumental to the presidential ambitions and disagreement within the party ADEMA-PASJ that led Keita to leave his position as Prime Minister. What is known is that Keita left ADEMA-PASJ in 2001 and created his own political party, Rally for Mali (RPM). He declared his candidacy at the presidential election in 2002. Mande Sidibe replaced Keita who remained in office and organized the presidential election in which Amadou Toumani Toure, the head of the transitional government, won the election. Women under Mande Sidibe gained more ministerial positions and new women made their presence in political leadership positions in Mali. There were seven ministerial positions allocated to women and at the same time, the ministerial positions increased with the creation of new offices. The Government of Mali

---

[72] Aminata Dramane Traoré. Une révoltée altermondialiste 21 mai 2008, Bamako (Mali). Propos recueillis par Sadou Yattara et Anne Perrin retieved 4/15/13 http:// www.oecd.org/fr/csao/publications/41682765.pdf. p3

under Mande Sidibe was composed of twenty-one ministers with seven women.

- 2000-02 Minister of Social Development, Solidarity and the Elderly: Mrs. Diakite Fatoumata Ndiaye

- 2000-02 Minister of Communications: Mrs. Ascofaré Ouleymatou Tamboura

- 2000-02 Minister for the Advancement of Women, child and family: Mrs. Diarra Afoussatou Thiero.

- 2000-02 Minister of Industry, Trade and Transport: Mrs. Touré Alimata Traoré.

- 2000-02 Minister for Health: Ms. Fatoumata Traoré Nafo.

- 2000-02 Minister of Handicrafts and Tourism: Mrs. Zakyatou Oualett Halatine.

- 2000-02 Minister of State areas and Land Affairs: Mrs. Bouaré Fily Sissoko.

The Minister of Communications, Mrs. Ascofaré Ouélématou Tamboura, resigned from the government in 2001 which engendered a small reshuffling of the government and the merging of the Ministry of Communications and of the Ministry of State Areas and Land Affairs under the leadership of Mrs. Bouaré Fily Sissoko. Conversely, certain ministries had been the domain of women since they had made their first appearance in the government which could be argued in different terms. In addition, what seems important here is the increase of the number of women in the political leadership position and the role they play on the political scene.

The strong tension that dominated the political scene in Mali between the major political party and the rest of the parties gradually started to fade away due to the organization of the national political forum. The forum was organized on January 1999 and led to the elaboration of a new electoral law for the country. In the 2002 presidential and legislative elections, all political parties started participating in the elections. It is also to explain that the president Alpha Oumar Konare was finishing his second and last term in office as established by the Malian Constitution. Even though there were no women candidates in the presidential race, there were a significant number of women in the legislative elections. Not to mention that among the twenty-five candidates in the race for president, the Constitutional Court rejected the candidacy of Mrs. Sidibe, Awa Sanogo for lack of payment of her fees. A chemist by profession, Awa was not encouraged by the results of ten years of revolution in the country vis-à-vis the women and tried to improve the status of women by running for president in the 2002 election in Mali. She was an independent candidate and member of the Malian Association for the Defense of Victims of Repression called (ADVR). Mrs. Sidibe, Awa Sanogo aimed to help everyone from her leadership once she accessed the supreme power of the country.

Unlike different other men in a patriarchal society, Awa's husband supported her to run for president as an independent candidate. As an argument against the rejection of her candidacy, Awa poignantly confirmed that she had already paid her nomination deposits of 5 million francs CFA (about $10,000) and had the support of her husband to run for president (Afrique Express 2001). Unfortunately, the only woman, who was supposed to make history as the first woman candidate, did not have the right to run in 2002 presidential election in the country. It was a few years later that another woman would run as a candidate at the presidential election in Mali and became the first woman to run for president. In the same token, if the number of women who run for president is not encouraging, the number of women in the ministerial cabinet, however, is comforting. In addition, looking at the names of different women that assumed ministerial positions, one would realize that the same names appeared several times. This led the reader to understand that even though the political leadership was open to women it was not an opportunity for any woman.

After Amadou Toumani Toure's election as president of the fourth republic, more women started enjoying political leadership roles in the country in the government under Prime Minister Ahmed Mohamed Ag Hamani. Prime Minister Ag Hamani was not a novice on the Malian political scene due to his long past experience with

Moussa Traore's dictatorial regime that reigned over the country for more than two decades. He remained in office for two years and during his time, despite his experience on the political scene, he had only two women in his first government which was reshuffled a few months later within the same year. Prime Minister Mohamed Ag Hamani had three women ministers among the twenty-one Ministers that served in his government.

- 2002-04 Minister of Social Development, Solidarity and the Elderly: Mrs. N'Diaye Fatoumata Coulibaly (old).

- 2002-04 Minister of Social Development, Solidarity and the Elderly: Mrs. N'Diaye Fatoumata Coulibaly (old).

- 2002-02 Minister of Health: Mme Traoré Fatoumata Nafo (old).

- 2002-04 Minister of Health Mrs. Kéita, Rokiatou N'Diaye (new).

- 2002-04 Promotion of Women, Children and Family: Mrs. Berthé Aïssata Bengaly (new).

There were seven Minister Delegates having the rank of Minister with no woman. Despite women's presence in the political leadership position in Mali, there were still concerns about their roles in the government.

Under Prime Minister Ousmane Issoufi Maiga there were five ministries allocated to women regarded on the political scene as non-significant in women's progress in political leadership positions when people referred back to the number of women in the previous governments and the size of the actual government.

- 2004-2007 Mme Ba Hawa Keita Minister of Employment and Vocational Training.

- 2004-2007 Mme Diallo M'Bodji Sene, Minister of the Promotion of Women, Children and Family.

- 2004-2007 Me Fanta Sylla, Minister of Justice.

- 2004-2007 Mme Soumare Aminata Sidibe, Minister of Government Real Estate and Land.

- 2004-2007 Mme Maiga Neinab Mint Youba, Minister of Health.

This enthusiasm of women to join politics in mass was somehow encouraged by western donors that wanted to see more women on the political scene enjoying political leadership positions. In addition, based on the Malian social values and beliefs, this encouragement by western forces for women to enjoy political leadership did not go without bringing tensions in the society, particularly in families. Conversely, even though the number of women was increasing, this increase was not static due to the fact that women's representation in the leadership position was not at a constant rate. Some have indicated that this attitude of the government brought the attention of donors about women's involvement in political activities. The inconsistency to maintain more women in the government could be seen within all government in Mali; it was not the government led by Modibo Sidibe that would make an exception to this rule. After Ousmane Maiga Issoufi submitted his resignation and that of his government on 27 September 2007, Modibo Sidibe replaced Prime Minister Maiga. This nomination of Modibo Sidibe was instrumental to the re-election of Amadou Toumani Toure for a second and last term in office.

As discussed earlier, it was in the 2007 election that the first woman candidate had the right to run for president. Some argued that the candidacy of Mrs. Sidibe, Aminata Diallo of the Rally for Sustainable Education and Development political party, was a result of Western partners' pressure on Mali. The irony here was that the political party of Mrs. Sidibe, Aminata Diallo created around the election period stopped its activities or disappeared once the elections were over and she became Minister of Basic Education, Literacy, and the National Languages. Mrs. Diallo is an academic and politician and a member of the Faculty of Economic Sciences and Management at the University of Bamako. The political agenda she had when she was running against Amadou Toumani Toure for president, was for a sustainable environment and environmental protection. As a major public concern about Mrs. Diallo's candidacy, people continued to ask themselves about the seriousness of her candidacy and they also wondered how an oppositional presidential candidate could easily join the government even though she knew that the elected president presented different agendas for the country. In the first government, Amadou Toumani Touré after his election for his second and last term in office, there were 26 ministers appointed under Prime Minister Modibo Sidib. The first Government counted twenty-seven ministers including seven women, in September 28, 2007.

- 2007-09 Minister of Cattle and Fisheries, Diallo Madeleine Bâ.

- 2007-08 Minister of Economy, Industry and Commerce, Bâ Fatoumata Néné Sy.

- 2007-09 Minister of Basic Education, Alphabetisation and the National Languages, Sidibé Aminata Diallo.

- 2007-09 Minister of Promotion of Women, Children and the Family, Maiga Sina Damba.

- 2007-09 Minister of Communication and the New Technologies, Diarra Mariam Flantié Diallo.

- 2007-09 Minister of Housing and Urbanism, Gakou Salimata Fofana.

- 2007-09 Minister charged with Relations with Institutions and Government Spokesperson, Diabaté Fatoumata Guindo.

Mrs. Ba Fatoumata Nene Sy stayed in office for a short period and was later removed from the Minister of Economy, Industry and Commerce by President Toure and replaced by Amadou Abdoulaye Diallo. According to several sources in Mali, this departure was not a surprise for anyone in Mali based on political differences. However, the number of women in the second government of Prime Minister Modibo Sidibe was not consistent in increasing the number of woman ministers after the 2009 reform. This inconsistency explains the decrease of the number of woman ministers after President Amadou Toumani Touré reshuffled the Government of Modibo

Sidibé on April 9, 2009. The new government counted 30 ministers with six women.

- 2009-11 Minister of Livestock and Fisheries, Diallo Madeleine Ba.

- 2009-11 Minister for the Promotion of Women, Children and Families, Maiga Sina Damba.

- 2009-11 Minister of Communication and New Technologies, Mme Diarra Mariam Diallo Flantié.

- 2009-11 Minister of Housing, Land Affairs and Planning, Mme Gakou Salamah Fofana.

- 2009-11 Minister of Higher Education and Scientific Research, Siby Ginette Bellegarde.

- 2009-11 Minister in charge of Relations with Institutions, Spokesperson of the Government Mme Diabaté Fatoumata Guindo.

In 2009, Amadou Toumani Toure reshuffled the government and retained Modibo Sidibe as Prime Minister and replaced the Minister of Basic Education, Alphabetisation and the National Languages, Sidibé Aminata Diallo. A new woman Mrs. Siby Ginette Bellegarde joined the government as the Minister of Higher Education and Scientific Research. This reshuffle led to reducing the number of women in the government from seven to six. For a long time, the number of woman ministers that was increasing went down rapidly and this continued with the nomination of a woman as Prime Minister of the country.

So far on the political scene in Mali, the head of the government had always been men but women would make their debut as prime minister in 2011. Even though this nomination was just a façade showing to the world how women are progressing on the political scene, it was encouraging for women to see a woman Prime Minster for the first time. She did not have real power as well as her predecessor men under the Amadou Toumani Toure's presidency who was the one making decisions. Prime Minister

Sidibé resigned on March 30, 2011 and was replaced by Cissé Mariam Kaïdama Sidibé. On April 3, 2011 she was announced as Prime Minister with 33 ministers including the Premier Minister Mrs. Cissé Mariam Kaïdama Sidibé. Despite the increase in the number of ministers, the number of women in leadership positions did not experience a growth.

- 2011-12 Ministre of Health, Mrs. Diallo Madeleine Bâ.

- 2011-12 Minister of Industry, Investment and Commerce, Mrs. Sangaré Niamoto Ba.

- 2011-12 Minister of Higher Education and Scientific Research, Mrs. Siby Ginette Bellegarde.

- 2011-12 for the Promotion of Women, Children and Families, Dr. Konaré Mariam Kalapo, replaced in 2012 by Dandara Touré.

Even though the president Amadou Toumani Toure started by nominating more women in the ministerial positions and appointed a first woman Prime Minister in the history of Mali, the number or women in the different government cabinets during Toure's presidency continued to decrease. The irony here is that the number of women also did not increase in the government under Prime Minister Mrs. Cisse. Prime Minister Mrs. Cisse experienced the record of the lowest number of women in the government under Amadou Toumani Toure's presidency. Women representation in this government continued to remain the same, and Mrs. Konate Dandara Touré replaced Dr. Konaré Mariam Kalapo the Minister for the Promotion of Women, Children and Families on February, 16 2012 (Mali archives).

They considered the different ministerial positions allocated to women as symbolic, but did not give women any real power in decision-making. Importantly, if certain people argue that women did not play any serious leadership role in the different governments in Mali and their number was non-significant on the political scene as argued by Fanta Diarra interviewed by Djibril Sacko (July 30, 2007), one should argue that the Ministry of Employment responsibilities were not easy tasks at a time of social unrest in the country.

CHAPTER V
••

WOMEN AND POLITICAL LEADERSHIP

Women Political Leaders:
Their Characterizations and Political Views

This chapter deals with women's role in politics and what they think about political leadership. In order to understand the types of leadership on the political scene in Africa, and mainly in Mali, about women's political leaders it will be significant to listen to their stories about their political participation in their respective countries. Many issues, such as a woman's role in contemporary African politics, women's liberation and politics, women's political and social advancement, women's opinion about politics, women's political achievements, solidarity between women, women and the politics of self-promotion, women and the politics of change, women and political gains, women and political adversities, women as political leaders appear in women's political discourse.

Women's Role in Contemporary African Politics

The contemporary African political scene deals with the different roles played by women political leaders made of hopes and despairs. At the end of the colonial oppression that led to independence in Africa, most women started looking at politics differently, with a critical mind. They stopped seeing men as the sole actors in the public arena, and they became increasingly involved in political exercises. There were successful collaborations between women and men, even though there were still questions about the leadership role played by women such as Aoua Keita in Mali. However, different people have argued in the favor of women that their political involvement has brought remarkable progress, not only in their lives but also in the lives of their family and community. In addition, women's current participation in politics and the role they have played as political leaders has brought changes in the continent despite the fact some have adopted different attitudes toward these observations with precaution. Based on women's opinions about politics, such as the President of Liberia, Helen Johnson Sirleaf, their political involvement can bring tremendous change in their own lives and in the society they live in. This argument is essentially based on the type of leadership women bring on the political scene, as they say in Bamanan: *ni ye Muso kelen kalan, i ye kabila kelen kalan, i ye jamana kelen kalan* (meaning that when you educate a woman you educate a whole community and a whole country). This comment based on women education is also pertinent to women on the political scene. In the same tone, this statement is a justification of world organizations' interest in women programs throughout the world, especially in Africa: namely their presence on the political scene as key players.

In a general sense, democracy seems to offer some signs of encouragement to women. Women use the political podium to talk on the behalf of those in the countryside who were considered to be the pillars of the society especially during political campaigns. In their argument, women in the remote areas have contributed much and benefit less from the state services. The same women politicians suggest that their work should be based on how to better help and celebrate less privileged women working on farms. They claim in the following statement that women in the rural areas do not merit any disdain:

It is therefore unfair to repair from the point of view of perception rather than from reality. Women who gave their all to Mali are in the countryside, that corner that some contemptuous minds call the "bush." We need to think about these women and pay tribute to them all. They have never experienced the luxury and comfort, the rhetoric and political calculation, their whole life has been labor and childbirth, often in appalling conditions. These are the women to look for and to celebrate.

Based on such arguments about women, certain groups come to the realization of their tremendous contribution in the society. In the work done by certain women leaders, such as Aoua Keita of Mali, Joyce Banda of Malawi, Mrs Sira Diop of Mali, Aminata Dramane Traore of Mali, Helen Sirleaf Jonhson of Liberia, Saudatu Shehu Mahdi of Nigeria, Najatu Mohammad of Nigeria, Samiah Nkrumah of Ghana, Bernadette Lahai of Sierra Leone, a common thread in their leadership and activism was the desire to honor African women in their everyday struggle. Women political leaders today see themselves as the voice of those women living in the rural areas, disregarded by the rest of the population and especially the politicians. Nowadays, rural women comprehend that they become a center of interest during election time when politicians are in their quest for a vote, due to their great numbers living in the dungeon of despair. However, rural women's rich numbers does not help them in their struggle for political progress. Instead of benefiting from their number in becoming a leading force in politics, despite their protest, women are used as a distraction as discussed by Kofo Bucknor-Akerele at the 7th annual Trust Dialogue in Abuja:

In order to appease these women, some political parties divide the instrument of women's wings. Most cases, the women's wings were formed mainly to provide entertainment and refreshment at the campaign rallies of the men, and of course to mobilize other women to vote for the men. These women's wings were reduced to singing, dancing and clapping instruments to boost the political campaign of the men.

In this statement, Bucknor-Akerele points out the unenviable role women play on the political scene in the continent despite the undeniable contribution they brought on the political scene. Knowing that in most multiparty democratic systems the candidate with the most votes wins the election, it becomes who gets what, how much and at what cost. Based on this phenomenon in politics, women start asking for more equitable share of the political power. In the quest of political leadership, it should be taken into account the dichotomy between the oppressed and the oppressor discussed by Paulo Freire. For Paolo Freire, the struggle engaged by the oppressed for equality sometimes might lead to a desire of the oppressed to envy the position of the oppressor. This further explains the attitudes of free slaves in Liberia and the Europeans that fled oppression in Europe for the American continent. There are presently women on the political scene, who are vying for the leadership position instead of trying to play a role in the community.

On the other hand, some women tend to accept the idea that they are not part of the political activities due to the preconceived idea they have about political leadership being male-oriented, as Dr Rose Mensah-Kutin from the ABANTU for Development states:

> Originally when you think of a leader you think of a very big person, you think of somebody who has to be obeyed, you think of a leader also in masculine terms. And so immediately women [in Ghana] feel that that is not a space for them and they are also made to feel that way.[73]

The role undertaken by women on the social scene is regarded as secondary even though they continue to prove their talents in politics. As an example of prejudices is the "customary" laws that

---

[73] Dzodzi Tsikata and Akosua K. Darkwah from the Pathways of Women's Empowerment: What are we Learning? Conference, 20 – 24 January 2009.

gave African men, particularly males elites, advantages over women in questions of divorce and marriage.[74] Many women, as well as men give credit to these social prejudices, which continue to hamper their progress in political leadership positions by supporting men's agenda and not seeing politics in the optics of liberation.

Women's Liberation and Politics

Politics is seen as a liberating force from the yoke of social, political and economic constraints. African women political activists have for a long time played key roles in different social changes, even though some did not directly address their causes. Instead of being involved in the fight for their progress, many joined the global fight for either independence or patriotism. Despite their dedication to the fight for national causes, women remain oppressed on the political arena (Geisler, 2004).

One reason for the slow start to women's rights activism may be that women, who focused their activism on their progress, were often targeted as threats to the social order. Women activists such as Bernadette Lahai of Sierra Leone, Mrs Sira Diop and several other African women activists fought for the cause of women. Unlike those women leaders mentioned earlier, Aoua Keita focused her activism on the liberation and the freedom of the oppressed throughout the world. She poignantly stated that:

Political independence was the great culmination of our efforts and sacrifices of our martyrs… the fight was not over, however. It continues and will continue for a long time for freedom, democracy and universal peace.[75]

In this context, Keita emphasized the complementarity between men and women, instead of the relationship between oppressed and oppressor as it was represented by certain other political activists.

---

[74] Kathleen Sheldon (Aug 2013). Women and Colonialism. Oxford Bibliographies in African Studies Publication
[75] Keita, A. (1975). *La vie d'Aoua Keita racontee par elle-meme"*, an autobiography. Paris: Presence Africaine.p395

The experience of Aoua Keita on the political scene was marked by the collaboration she developed with men politicians in the struggle for independence.

Even though certain women politicians had difficulty conveying their political involvement, they considered politics as a tool of empowerment. Based on this awareness, many women activists in the continent seized the political debate podium for empowerment. Mrs Sira Diop used the political platform to defend women's agenda through the adoption of a new Family Code that was in debate in Mali in 2009. She argued that the adoption of a new Family Code was going to bring tremendous change by increasing women's rights in the Malian society. It is the same change discussed by Mrs Diop that led many women in the continent to become involved in politics. In addition, for illiterate and Muslim women who are submissive to their husbands, one can understand their reactions vis-à-vis the text being against the principles of their tradition and the Islamic values. But if it was to be promulgated, their reaction to a new Family Code in Mali might have differed from the one of intellectual women activists. Nonetheless, the importance for women leaders was that the new code would push more women to emancipate themselves and take control of their destiny. Importantly, this new Family Code stipulates the separation of property between spouses when monogamy is an advanced form, having more than two wives. In the past, what the wife earned belonged to her husband. If a man was indebted to his wife, it was canceled due to the custom and if it was the opposite, the woman remained indebted to her husband. These situations, related to tradition, minimized the status of women. Therefore, this new code was considered to be a step forward for women, even if the change of mentality was slow to function as supported by Mrs Sira Diop.

The involvement of many intellectuals in politics today is due to the effort of women to change the way political affairs were carried out in the continent. It is also important to underline that that has not been the case during the European colonial presence in the country as supported by different sources in Africa. The attitude of intellectual women in the past was presented as a group of silent people that paid little attention to political activities, despite the encouragement of women leaders. Educated women at a certain level in most African countries under Europeans' colonial oppression manifested less interest in politics, and they remained sidelined, despite their level of education and knowledge about the issue at stake. They hardly wanted to play a part in politics despite their long history of working alongside men in politics. In addition to traditional social roles restricting women's participation, women may also deliberately avoid politics due to their perception that it is a difficult and dirty game.

Intellectual women's inaction in leadership was used by some women activists as an argument against women activists to discourage them from political activity. Activists such as Aoua Keita (1908-1984), Yaa Asantewaa (1850-1921) the Queen Mother of an Asante state of Ghana and many others tried to free the continent from colonial oppressive forces by allowing Africans to be in charge of their own destiny. On the other hand, the hard work of women alongside men in the struggle for independence made them overlook their own issues, but that male leaders did not make room for women's issues in their progressive politics. They were considered less important. Women were disillusioned because the fight for liberation turned out to be more for men as Geisler (2004) points out:

> Even though women entered early nationalist movements with a hope of liberating their country and also themselves, nationalist leaders failed to acknowledge women's oppression not only under colonialism but also under patriarchy.[76]

Women in these terms were not only oppressed by the colonial forces but also by their own social customs. Despite these challenges, many women have found reasons today to become actively involved in

---

[76] Gisela G. Geisler (2004). Women and the Remaking of Politics in Southern Africa: Negotiating Autonomy, incorporation and representation. Nordiska Africainstitutet publication. p64

politics and this motivation compels them to vie for political leadership positions across the continent for the benefit of their society.

Women's Political and Social Advancement

Social advancement being a difficult terminology to define in this context based on the different arguments from women about the topic, it will therefore be important to look at the definitions as they are used in political discourse, but especially as used by Malian women. When women were asked about their political agenda, the term 'social advancement' appeared to be the leitmotif of their political driving force. Social advancement here has been defined as a way to make everyone benefit from the national wealth or services. Certain women attested that once they joined politics their personal and social condition had improved considerably; such that they were able to afford so many things that they could not think about before the democratic event. While some women politicians tried to avoid addressing the question directly, one respondent, Dado, talked about what politics had brought to her in terms of personal gain:

> You see with politics, I gained a land that I sold for [a few] millions to pay the educations of my [child]. I told myself if I had money before I was not going to send my children to public schools but to send them all to private schools and to ensure them a better condition. (From direct conversation with Dado, August 2007).

It is mainly on the political scene that people can notice certain rapid improvement in politicians' social conditions. African women today are more than ever determined to be in political leadership positions and have an equitable share of responsibility with men in the society. They know that in order to reach that goal they will need to have a law that is evenhanded and that can to some extent defend women. What women found intolerable today in most of the African countries is the fact that the house chores are considered as women's sole responsibility that hinder their social and educational advancement (Nana Oye Lithur EWB-conversation 2010). Nana continues discussing that the dichotomy in this complaint is that the majority of women became an indefectible accomplice of their man in general and reinforced the same role on young girls' vis-à-vis young boys.

In the past few years, the question about the protection of women has made an echo throughout the world due to its urgency such at the 1995, Fourth World Conference on Women in Beijing and the 2010, 7th annual Trust Dialogue in Abuja. African women's social condition has for a long time brought discussions on the national and international scenes. The internationalization of the debate about women's issues has been the driving force that has given some women the courage to stand up and fight for themselves against any form of violence and abuse. In this fight against violence or mistreatment against women, Najatu Mohammad of Nigeria, Aoua Keita of Mali, the president Joyce Banda of Zimbabwe, among others, challenged the social order in their respective countries and fought abuse against women struggling for their rights in a male-dominated society. Despite the improvement of the social conditions of women, they still believe that they face more obstacles on their way to political leadership. Winnie Mandela summarized this situation this way:

> We are seeing more equitable laws that are protecting women from discrimination abuse and violence, however there is much more that needs to be done to put the platform from action into practice especially in terms of alleviating poverty, improving health, creating opportunities for economic advancement and political leadership (2010, 7th annual Trust Dialogue in Abuja).

In general, the majority of African women prefer to experience a total improvement of their social conditions rather than simply seeing more women in political leadership positions in Africa.

However, there is another group of women such as Ellen Johnson Sirleaf, Samia Nkrumah, Mrs. Sira Diop, and Bernadette Lahai who believe that in order to see change in women's conditions, they need to be represented at the political leadership level. The necessity to have women in leadership positions in politics is explained by different researchers as instrumental to their social and political conditions.

In the past, if African women were fully participating in the social activities within the traditional society, this freedom of women was restrained because of twofold events that succeeded each other in Mali, which was similar to many other countries in Africa. The presence of Islam and the colonial oppressive forces in the continent were the two major forces that made little opening for women on the social scene. In the direct conversation with Oumou Sankare, she poignantly attests that her fellow women live in uphill conditions and that both their political and social conditions need some improvement. The argument of Oumou Sankare has been supported by other different women activists in Mali in the early fight for independence.

In general, despite the fear for certain women to take risk on the political scene and their disdain for political animosity, some women still believe that it is worthwhile to persevere in the pursuit of increased political representation for women. It is this same ambition, however, that has made some women politicians vulnerable to manipulation by others in politics with their own agendas. Mrs Djire recalled that:

> I was trying to become a mayor, it did not work, and I tried to be at the high council of the collectivity that did not work. During the past legislative election, I submitted my documents, it did not work. If I am still lucky, I will continue trying. In 2002, there was a (political party) group that came to see me so that I could become their candidate for the legislative elections. They told me that if it was a question of money, that they were ready to finance my campaign.

> Me, I did not have anything (money). When people
> called me, I said to myself that one does not refuse
> an honor. (From direct conversation with Mrs Djire,
> August 2007).

This statement demonstrates how some women have understood through their experience as an activist that they need some kind of self-determination, not dependence on the financing of others, to reach their goals. Najatu Mohammad added that:

> Women going into politics, must go in with a clear
> cut vision, with a goal and an objective, unwavering
> objective; as what they want and what they want to
> become.

In spite of the degree of accuracy in this statement, it will be important to see if the majority of women on the political scene share this vision of Mohammad. In the same vain, the subordination of women and not their equality to men, lead several women to discouragement. For a great number of African women, politicians have not demonstrated anything that they can rely on. They, therefore, rebel against the new social order designed for them and that they find today unacceptable.

Women's Opinion about Politics

Women's opinion about politics deals with the way they perceive politics as political leaders. Observing politics in the general African context, it is regarded as a pitiless private domain of men that has no room for women no matter how they look at politics. Women have always proven that politics has not been a new thing for them despite the switch of terminologies. They argue that they have been playing political roles in their different societies in a successful manner which has had its impact on things such as politics, economy, and organizations. Sweetman explains that:

...women have set up thousands of vibrates, visionary organizations of their own, which have had considerable success in influencing the policy of governments, international financial institutions, and development agencies over the past 30 years.[77]

Despite the mysteries that encompass politics, African women happen to join it and reach the leadership positions. The move of women toward political leadership has been motivated by different social, political, and economic reasons. In the introduction of her book, Sheldon supports women's political move stating that the "Analysis of the development of legal systems under colonialism suggests that women were at a disadvantage, as "customary" laws were established based on male testimony that gave men, especially elite men, advantages over women in issues of marriage and divorce. Women's precolonial political activity was generally disregarded by the colonial authorities, who turned exclusively to men when they established local political offices."[78] If the African women's political debut has been inspired by different reasons, their first experience on the political scene has not been stress-free. Discussing their political debut, several women confirmed that at their debut they had discomfort speaking before a crowd that they believed were the realm of men. They found political activities difficult, even though some were teachers and were already used to talking before a large classroom of students. Teaching, however, prepares people to activities such as speaking before a crowd that is a key component of politics despite the dissimilarity between these two activities. The timidity of certain women politicians was considered an act of embarrassment due to the mystification of the political scene as it is stated by Oumou Sankare:

> I said at the beginning that I could not speak in front of people that I was ashamed...so far there are times

---

[77] Sweetman, C.(2000) Women and Leadership. Oxfam, GB. p2
[78] Kathleen Sheldon (Aug 2013). Women and Colonialism. Oxford Bibliographies in African Studies Publication. p38

that I feel ashamed. (From the direct conversation
with Oumou Sankare August 2007).

This state of mind hinders the majority of women politicians'
activism before they become accustomed to the political scene.
Hardships in politics can explain this discomfort of certain women
politicians as described by certain people as the 'animosity' between
politicians. These hardships are very often from women toward other
women based on the fact that one candidate happens to win an election
instead of another one. According to many women politicians, this
attitude between women has engendered harsh competition among
candidates. The fight between candidates has not deviated women
from their goal to help their sisters. They see politics as a way to bring
what is necessary for the rest of women in order to satisfy their needs.

> We really want to help our sisters all the time. We
> can really help women either at the low level or at
> the communal level. (From direct conversation with
> Oumou Sankare, August 2007).

Despite the lack of clarification about the type of help, women
seem to show their determination in assisting other women. This
argument from a majority of women was considered as a counter
argument about promises women used to receive from men on the
political scene that had hardly been delivered as Oumou Sankare
attested that they "promise" it but do not keep their word. However,
women leaders show their attachment to the trepidations of other
women by having constant meetings with them and trying to have
their telephone numbers. This was, indeed, a way to keep a close
relationship with their constituency. The action of women politicians
trying to protect and provide for other women is considered a way
of political opportunity and potential vote to gain. This political
calculation is what women leaders try to safeguard other women
from becoming victim of the political game based on who gets what,
how, how much and at what cost.

Conversely, the attitude of certain women acting as protectors of their sisters is seen as a way of making other women do what they want them to do like most of the leadership theorists fear, vis-à-vis charismatic leaders. Charismatic leaders sometimes use their charisma to make followers do what he/she wants them to do. The argument here is that women activists try to demarcate themselves from those who fail to address the need of the community. It is not uncommon to hear certain women talking about specific political positions as more profitable compared to others that bring fewer advantages and enjoyment to politicians.

> I am at ease with my teaching profession. Well, as far as the position of mayor is concerned, I am at ease with it too even though we do not have an important position (laughter). What do you think; I do not know how to say it. We are not at the top in this office. We do not have a communal office. Those are the good positions *o lu de ka wusa o*. Those are very important positions we are not included in any of those *an t'o si la*. And with politics too, even though we are having an important position (she laughs). We are not on top of a communal office. Those are the important positions *o lu de ka wusa*. We are not in any of those *an t'o si la*. We are just city councilwomen. (From direct conversation with Bintou Sidibe, August 2007).

This explains a desire for political positioning among them at specific political key positions in order to gain the maximum profit, hence their regret for losing strategic locations. The negative attitude on the political scene has brought women activists to try to redefine their political engagement.

Many women activists accentuate the leadership role played by women to be different from the one played by men. They argue that their political engagement must not be restricted to the fact that they see politics as an eternal triangle of business rather than to incorporate the real debate about political activities. Women strongly state that anything concerning them should come from them and not from any other source. A similar argument has been supported by Winnie Mandela at the African Women and Politics the 7th Annual Trust Dialogue that was held in Abuja, Nigeria in these terms:

> I need to emphasize this point; our engagement should not be limited to the business of politics but should extend to discussion about the politics of business (2010).

The participation of women in political decision-making becomes more important now than ever to reach the goal they have set for themselves in the society. Women further use the political platform to reach out to one another to reflect on their realizations and feebleness. In opposition, what women in political leadership positions have found as a threat to their survival in politics is to try to pretend that they are someone that they are not. Women political activists such as Mrs. Sira Diop, Aminata Dramane Traore, Winnie Mandela, and Wangari Maathai would exhort women to believe in themselves in order to change their social, political, economic and cultural realities. In her political speech in Abuja, Winnie Mandela points out how they should seize the opportunity given to them in these terms:

> This platform should give us an opportunity to pose difficult questions as well as to reflect on our achievements and weaknesses while we also come up with ideas on how best to approach the issue of gender parity and enhance the quality of our contribution in the critical agents of our various economy (2010, 7th annual Trust Dialogue in Abuja).

The argument is that women are not questioning their leadership skills or competencies; however, they are cognizant about the challenges and obstacles on the political scene. The analogue argument about women leaders has been supported by different researchers on the field which showed no doubt about the confidence in their leadership capabilities. Klenke (1996) stated that:

> Women leaders do not lack confidence in their leadership abilities nor the competence to function effectively as leaders, but they experience a sense of tokenism, vulnerability, and precariousness.[79]

The argument of women activists is that their competence cannot be denied, but their long-time political suppression led them to lose confidence in their abilities to bring about change. Based on the following experience, most woman politicians try to reproduce the model displayed by men on the political scene, not taking into consideration that such models defend a different agenda as Winnie Mandela states:

> Be honest as a candidate; don't try to be something you are not fitting in a suit that just does not fit... women were trying to fit in the industry that was designed in many ways to keep them out. Fight back (2010, 7th annual Trust Dialogue in Abuja).

The main way women believe to reach their goal as discussed by women activists and political leaders is through a struggle and fairness. They were equipped with a sense of justice and dignity.

> All of those women that come to see me or all of those people that come to see me, if I can solve their problem, I will solve it without a word. That was what my brother said. He said that I cannot benefit anything from the city hall because I am not a bandit. He said that to my son that I do not benefit anything (direct conversation with Bintou Sidibe, August 2007).

---

[79]   Klenke, K. (1996). Women and Leadership: A Contextual Perspective. Springer Publishing Company. New York. p17

Politicians in the African continent have been for a long time considered these unscrupulous people willing to do anything that does not dignify their person. Such statements about politics is not merely gender-based even though some women politicians acknowledge this statement about politics. However, they discuss that networking is more important than the material gain for women in politics. As it is confirmed in this statement:

> Well, when I was a teacher, there were certain things I could not do. But today, being a woman politician with contacts that one should not forget in politics, when I have difficulties sometimes I go see someone I knew through politics, he will not refuse his help. I think that contact is more important than money. (From direct conversation with Bintou Sidibe, August 2007).

Certain women politicians look at politics as any other social activity that once an individual joins it, she acquires a test for it and she will try to reach the next rank. This argument is supported by Oumou Sankare in a direct conversation saying that:

> It is like a school. You start in first grade you go to second grade. One must progress." (From direct conversation with Oumou Sankare, August 2007).

The argument about whether women's type of leadership is different from the leadership style of men has always brought discussion among women. The main reason that women could not come up with answers for this argument is that they find the question at the same time important and complicated to answer. Nevertheless, several women leaders took a stand about the question by responding that women and men lead differently. Mark Whitaker, Washington Bureau Chief and Senior Vice President, NBC News May 25, 2010 asked a similar question to President

Ellen Johnson in these words: Do women lead differently? The response of President Johnson was:

> Yes...sensitivity to humankind...They work harder...
> they have always played a dual roles, they have carried
> the family...carried the job responsibility.

The response of President Johnson emphasizes the dissimilarity of leadership displayed by woman on the political scene vis-à-vis their counterpart men. Another argument about this difference has been discussed by several women activists that women on the social scene are constantly going through challenges to prove themselves in order to gain access to certain social or professional leadership positions as Trauth (2002) states in this passage:

> ...a woman has to prove herself over and over again
> whereas a male has instant credibility because of his
> sex (p.108).

This also explains the ongoing struggle of women on the political and social scene. Even though women believe in leading differently, there are still a good number of women who espouse the idea of having the same agenda as men politicians as discussed by Mrs. Djire:

> The program is a common program. Women do not
> have a different program. But it is the way of doing
> things which can make the difference. And, that is
> what I often say to the women during meetings. They
> must make the difference. If they do the same thing
> like men, they will not have the chance. If we follow
> the boss, everyone follows the boss in order to have
> his/her daily bread and we say nothing, then, where is
> the difference (meaning between men and woman).
> Why do men vote for you if it is the same thing? But,

when people understand that you fight for them, they can say now we no longer want a man president we want a woman president. (From direct conversation with Mrs Djire, August 2007).

In this argument, Mrs. Djire accentuates differences even though she supports a similarity of dealing with state affairs. Indeed, the struggle that seems to floor the main path to women's political participation and survival can hardly happen without a degree of visualization that will guide the action. In this passage, Bell Hooks (2000) tries to inspire women in proposing the type of adequate vision that women need in order to reach their goals:

> To be truly visionary, we have to root our imagination in our concrete reality while simultaneously imagining possibilities beyond that reality.[80]

Vision by itself is not sufficient if it does not inculcate rational thinking and action that will bring about unexpected results. In imagining these possibilities, some women leaders see politics as a school that one has to progress to the next level which should define their individual achievement.

Women's Political Achievements

Political achievement is explained as based on bilateral or multilateral cooperation between countries in which the state or the people are the main beneficiaries. It is also observed here as the positive role played by women leaders on a domestic or international scene. Conversely, political achievement has been in most of the African societies subject to who gets what, how much and at what cost. These concepts about politics appear to describe the behavior of many people on the political scene worldwide. Even though such a

---

[80]   Bell Hooks (2000). Feminism Is for Everybody. South End Press. p110

conception about politics worldwide has an equal effect on the way politics is defined in Africa, there is little attention given to personal contribution in the national sense. When we ask women leaders about their political achievements, they argue that they have not yet reached what they want to accomplish or project in the future things they hope to accomplish before they leave their position. Of course, many leaders discuss the improvement of their social and economic condition being their political progress as these statements point out:

> We try anyway to get the best out of it trying to take care of our family needs and trying to get children good conditions. Me, I regret why I did not get involved in politics sooner. Because when I was not involved in politics, I did not have the means (From direct conversation with Dado, August 2007).

> I do not have what I wanted. I wanted to have more. To be a minister; and who does not want to be a minister? Because I know that I cannot have a better position, than the position that I am having now…Because we are not in power (From direct conversation with Oumou Sankare, August, 2007).

Politics has helped many leaders to achieve their personal goals in the African continent; the more they realize they can achieve so much through politics, the more they begin to regret the time spent outside politics. In addition to personal achievement, there are leaders who discuss that the achievement is merely collective based on the fact that everyone on the political scene works on a common agenda and that the success should not be regarded personal.

There have been difficulties to separate personal achievement in the sense from political achievement to what one has accomplished on the behalf of a nation as well. The answer from most of the women political leaders in Mali about their political achievement is very often geared toward what they happened to accomplish for their family or themselves rather than their political achievement benefiting the community. This, however, does not negate the accomplishment of many women leaders toward their constituency or country.

Solidarity between Women

The main debate of women about building a solid community by conscientizing other women in order to face the real challenges they are encountering in different domains in their lives has always been the core component of their political activism. The argument of women on the political platform to display their difficulties in order to find a solution is very common in their discourse. Most of the women politicians in Africa, and mainly in Mali, have voiced their discontent about their situation and about laws that they believe to be unfriendly to women as explained here:

> Women are more miserable. Women depend on men. Women suffer too much. Have not you noticed that here? It is women who do all of the house chores. They are busy taking care of the children. At the same time, if the husband faces difficulties to provide money for the groceries, the woman tries to help him out. It does not matter if the woman has to go do people's laundries for some cash…Thus, there are women who suffer (From direct conversation with Oumou Sankare, August 2007).

The significance of these women's discourse has resonated at international and local meetings throughout the world. Especially, the Beijing Conference, which has strongly contributed to bringing to the attention of the world the concern of women that mobilized world leaders behind their agenda today. It is, therefore, based on the experience from those platforms organized on the behalf of women on the international scene that has contributed to the rise of more and more women political activists. Another key component in this matter is the different platforms and the urgency to become the main agent of their liberation that many women found the necessity of solidarity around the creation of different opportunities for women in general. From the direct conversation with Oumou Sankare she stated that:

> At that time, I was not member of a political party. I was a member of a woman association. There was a group of women; we were doing tontines (women get together and raise money that they give it to one person each time they meet) and others. I was a member of an Association (August 2007).

Women as independent entities try to come up with policies that can maintain and strengthen their solidarity on the political scene that they attempt to emerge on by relying on their own capacities and imagination. A woman politician such as the Ghanian Samia Nkrumah at the 7th Annual Trust Dialogue in Abuja discussed her solidarity towards women of her community in these terms:

> In order to increase access to credit in my small constituency, in South-West of Ghana, I have adopted a private company that is running a micro-economy scheme to give credit to women to help them begin small businesses.

Such little enterprises have been developed by women in different regions in the African continent and mainly in Mali. Many women see their political involvement as a necessity to strengthen solidarity between women on the political scene and to contribute to maintaining the cohesion even though these matters sometimes experience difficulties.

Imagine women talking about their experience of women's organizations to be a way of alleviating women's economic hardship; however, some women find the same woman organization a burden to carry. The argument of Oumou Sankare tells a dissimilar story about what many women think about women's associations. Some women feel that their role as facilitator for women's groups to have access to things such as leadership or loans put their credibility at risk in case they do not honor their engagement vis-a-vis the lender. Oumou Sankare discussed that she was a member of a woman association that was giving loans to women and it ended up in divergence. She continues arguing that some women are in debt and do not pay back their dues. Practically, the cosigner has to pay back the loan if the recipient fails to pay back the loan, which can affect the credibility of the leader. She informed her women's group in case they need to borrow money that they have to bring their identity card, personal contribution, and then she will ask community development banks to give them a loan. In order to have a clear understanding of the loan system, women asked her what would happen in case they fail to pay back the loan. The response to that question was the women's association would have to pay for the one who fails to honor her engagement. Oumou Sankare's question to the women was to encourage someone to volunteer as a leader of the group, yet everyone declined the proposition in these words: 'I do not want to be the leader.' This answer explains the complexity of leadership in its contexts.

When the responsibility becomes unbearable for many women politicians to help other women, they simply prefer to withdraw their support from their association they used to belong to. This attitude of woman leaders is seen as a way to incite in their followers' a certain sense of leadership and to become accountable for their own actions. In Mali, as argued by some women political leaders, many women followers believe that they can take advantage of politicians that are supposed to solve their personal issues by giving them in return their vote. The constituencies sometimes fail to understand that the struggle of the leader is to defend their common program as Samia Nkrumah points out:

> The call for economic self-reliance, social justice, national cohesion, and greater continental integration are quite special relevant today because sustainable economic development that impacts all of us but

especially our women and their development is still very much out of reach. A woman in parliament is crucial for our development agenda (2010, 7th annual Trust Dialogue in Abuja).

Considerably, the support of women politicians for their fellow women to help in ending their social, economic, and political situation tries to alleviate the notion of dependence and lack of responsibility. However, the different struggles of women activists have been for a long time centered on how to conscientize other women about the urgency of their solidarity and the importance of their political participation. Even though they sometimes find their effort ineffective on the political ground, they still believe that the success of their struggle will depend on their own resilience. Most of these arguments are contingent on the lack of having the same vision or real trust between leaders and the followers. Some women rely on the force that they represent in the society and the necessity to help women to use that force to their benefit and the one of the community while some women rely on personal benefit based on the cooperation with their leadership. Such a lack of understanding cannot go without creating a sense of frustration from the leadership. From the direct conversation with Mrs Djire, she emphasized lack of comprehension with her fellow women stating that:

> They do not understand anything that is going on here; they understand differently. In fact, all of those women who come to see me or all of those people who come to see me, if I can solve their problem (financially), I will solve it without a word. That was what my brother said. He said that I cannot benefit anything from the city hall because I am not a bandit. He said to my son that I do not benefit anything (August 2007).

Furthermore this situation explains that sometimes when a woman leader becomes aware of her responsibility or wants to do her job in order to benefit the masses, the reaction she receives from other women is not very often encouraging. Many followers think that a leader is supposed to manage public property as a personal belonging. However, if some leaders try to cling to power, there are many women who are ready to give away their position to another woman on the political scene. They do believe in the necessity of women solidarity, but it does not matter if it is politics that is commonly believed to be based on personal gain. A general assumption of women on the political scene in Africa is their willingness to leave their seat for another contestant. In a direct conversation with Bintou she states that: "I will give up [meaning her seat], I mean to another woman because everyone cannot be on the list." This statement has been supported by many women politicians in Mali. The argument here however is centered on the sacrifice women are willing to make on the political scene that gives them more credibility as leaders. Here, a pertinent argument about women solidarity is presented by Bintou:

> Yes, we are there to defend women's cause. For example, during the past elections, the lists that had more women candidates, we asked women to vote for those lists. As there are women associations, we ask women to vote for those lists...For example, there is a woman association which asks women, it even does commercials in neighborhoods asking, to vote for the lists that have more women candidates.

> As a woman, we want to help our sisters either on a low or high-level in the district. We can really help them. I am myself the chairperson of a commission at the communal level (from direct conversation with Bintou Sidibe, August 2007).

The existence of women's associations and organizations today have paved the way for women's political progress and solidarity even though this solidarity is supposed to be open to any group.

Women voting for women candidates rather than a program tend to promote women and reinforce their position, which is seen as a self-advancement benefiting one group or community and not the society. Conversely, women's ways of helping one another is sometimes at the expense of their own personal comfort:

> I am with women's organizations whenever they have social problems such as death, naming ceremonies, and marriages. I am with them because it is a social matter. I am a part of the *tontines* (it is explained as a group of women meeting on monthly or weekly basis, each person pay one amount of money and they give it to one person and so on and so forth) and other things. For example, even this morning a group of women told me that the *tontine* had restarted. I said that this time I cannot pay the full contribution because I have to pay my daughter in law's school fees. Mainly when we receive our salary, I pay for the whole month because I count only on my salary. Thus, I do that to show solidarity with the association if not I do not do it. But I did not want to single myself out either. I will pay only half; it is a little sum that will allow me to be part of the group (from direct conversation with Bintou, August 2007).

Indeed, several women leaders confirm that in order to establish a connection through networking between women, they are willing to sacrifice their personal comfort mainly their economy they have saved up. In addition, different weekly or monthly meetings organized by women's groups are considered to be opportunities to discuss their social, economic and political matters. It is during such meetings of women that they try to increase their awareness about their involvement in politics, and the problems they experience in their everyday life. Some women politicians try to use this event to their own benefit by searching for more support or by making the group do what they want them to do in order to realize their personal ambitions. Politics has been a tangible tool for many women to take possession of their matters and to promote their agenda.

Women and the Politics of Self-Promotion

Based on different arguments about African women's political leadership, researchers have shown that their reticence on the political scene in mass has maintained them at a lower rank in politics. Certain leadership theorists have proven that the absence of African women from political life and leadership is rooted in things such as their indefectible support to male leaders, which has hindered for a long time their political progress and social prosperity. Women for a long time had believed that supporting male leaders would help the whole community or society, but it turns out that in doing so women were keeping themselves away from the political leadership position and gave the opportunity to men leaders to use politics to their own advantage. As a consequence, women later realized that their absence and non-real involvement in political decision-making had caused them what they were experiencing in their different societies. With the democratic event, they found it imperative to join the political scene, this time in mass, and claiming leadership positions.

In many African countries, women took advantage of the democratic event in which they played important roles mainly in Mali for the fall of the military dictatorial regime. Women at first regrouped themselves under associations and organizations (*tonw* in Mali) as a solid force. These *tonw* later became political forces that they used in multiparty democratic elections to have voices. Women, in their quest for political leadership positions, have gained the support of international organizations that have sometimes pressured political parties in Africa about women participation as a condition to their assistance to the democratic system in the continent. In addition, even though this attitude of internal organization is seen with disdain by certain politicians in Africa, it has, therefore, increased the number of women in political leadership positions.

Many women today voice their appreciation toward the new democratic event in the continent that has given them more leadership positions. Most importantly, the determination of women in different leadership positions has encouraged their political involvement throughout the continent with a women president in Liberia and Malawi, women Prime Ministers in Burundi, Rwanda, Senegal, Mozambique, Madagascar, Mali, and Guinea-Bissau. There are many women today elected as members of parliament or appointed to higher leadership positions in Africa. This number is increasing considerably in different countries in the continent. Conversely, certain women have seen this action as an opportunity to women's self-promotion.

Some women explained their move to politics as instrumental to the profit one may gain. As explained by leadership theorists, several political leaders have the transactional leadership values; they are mainly on the political scene to make business deals. The argument about personal gain in politics is supported by Bintou in these statements:

> The reasons that led me to join politics, for me, anyway, there is a question of profit (meaning personal profit). There is a question of profit and a question of development to better help women. I am myself a leader of a women's group. If you are on the political scene you have facilities to manage certain problems more than when you are in education. We remain only in education. When you are a woman politician, in general, you have a lot of things to do without talking about women in the neighborhood (from direct conversation with Bintou, August 2007).

According to the same source, political promotion gives women all sorts of benefits that are the objective of the majority of women that join the political scene. In addition, they argue that almost all men join politics for the same motive, thus they are not willing to abandon their seats for women. Even though the question of profit has been a reality among women preoccupations, the social fabric in most of the African societies did not encourage women leadership. Several researchers have focused their study on the palpable contribution of women in the household, while many others have based their work on what women's involvement in politics can do to change a country.

Women and the Politics of Change

The quest for change has always been the main struggle for oppressed people for ages throughout the world, communities or groups that want to improve their conditions; and seeing women today in this position on the political scene testifies to this struggle. The majority of women on the political scene in Africa found their social situation unencouraging and voiced their discontent of this situation. In addition, most of the political parties even in the old democracies in the world are reluctant to entrust political leadership to defend women's agendas, based on their own personal reasons. However, the attitude of men vis-à-vis women in politics brought women to understand that a crucial way to improve or change their social status was through politics. In order to carry change, women tried to seize the democratic event in the continent to join politics despite the social and religious barriers. The result of women's interest in political leadership can be noticed everywhere throughout the African continent. If African women insist on arguing against inequality between men and women, they also see themselves as indefectible supports to their men. According to political leadership experts, (Sow, 2009) it is the combination of women's support of their men and the social burden that oppress African women.

There are several discourses about women in political leadership positions, particularly the type of leadership they will display on the political scene, but only a few of them pay more attention to the argument of women and how they see themselves as political leaders. The dialogue about women's political involvement has mainly been animated by the fear of certain obstacles in the social system that has reduced the role of women to the pillar of their society and the gatekeeper role in Africa. Thus, admitting this contribution of women by giving them more roles in political leadership positions will simply contribute to the progress and stability of any country.

In a general sense, women join the political scene to contribute to social change, and the majority of them as political activists explained their activism through the sense of solidarity that they share with their fellow women. In order for women to come up with initiatives that can bring progress within their different communities, they found it necessary to join forces. Some women argue that the progress they are talking about will not happen if there is a lack of thoughtful engagement behind a common objective, and it is that which has always delayed their advancement. This being an objective targeted by most of the women leaders; it will not become a reality unless they believe in their own strength as a pivotal force for their own emancipation. Winnie Mandela at the 7th Annual Trust Dialogue argued that:

> We can only build an unstoppable way of collective energy if we are able to reach out to one another. This principle holds to for women in politics. We are our own liberators and unity must bind expression in the way in which we approach our social, political, cultural, and economic development. This struggle like all struggles will have its own detractors. We will need to respond to our detractors with words that have also inspired our struggle to liberate us.

However, the motivation of women leaders to wage a common fight against the enemies for their social progress has been hijacked in some cases by those who are inspired by personal advantage. This action of some women leaders in politics has given a new direction to women political involvement, which is merely based on political gains.

Women and Political Gains

In a general sense, work has always been a source of sustainability, economic stability and social stability even though there are jobs that hardly meet those demands. Individuals and countries have always made visible what they have accomplished through work. However, when it comes to politics, the question of whether enrichment and influence gained through political activity can be seen as lawful gains is still an open question. Political figures are widely criticized for using their activities for personal benefit, and this has made many people skeptical of politics more broadly.

Politicians interviewed did not hesitate to discuss their income from political activity, especially the ways they invested it. Investing in their family has always been the most important word supported by these political leaders and some go further by explaining how they invested in their children:

> When my child failed his exam, I took my child to a private school. I sent him to a private school and after my child passed his exam, he went to University. While he was at the University he did another training that I paid from my pocket. You see with politics I was allocated a land that I sold…to pay the education of my child. I told myself if I had money before I was not going to send my children to public schools but to send them all to private schools, to surround them with special care (from direct conversation with Dado, August 2007).

The type of investment discussed by Dado can further explain the reality of politics and how far some leaders are willing to go to sacrifice the commonwealth for the welfare of their family while they are working for the people. It is also not rare to see women making comparisons between the attitude of other women and men on the political scene on the basis of personal investment. Many women in the African continent argue that once many men start making money, the first thing they think about is how to spend money on themselves, while women spend their money on the family. This argument has been supported by Najatu Muhammad, a Nigerian women activist at the African Women and Politics the 7th Annual Trust Dialogue and Joyce Banda the president of Malawi in the interview talk to Al Jazeera. According to Joyce Banda "Malawians deserve better" (June, 2012). Most of the women argue in the favor of making the best out of their political leadership and use the benefit in a constructive way. They discuss that they try 'anyway' to get the best out of politics trying to take care of their family needs giving to the children a better life. Some women go further explaining their disappointment of not getting involved in politics sooner because of what politics can bring to an individual. Dado stated that:

> Me, I regret not getting involved in politics before.
> Because when I was not involved in politics I did not
> have the means (August 2007).

Politics in this context is seen as the social apparatus that becomes inevitable for anyone regardless of gender, race or age to use in order to reach an objective. Even though some women complained about politics, it has, therefore, helped many other women to climb the social ladder. Thus, even though this argument is supported by many African women considering politics as a game based on personal gain, that has not been the case for Oumou Sankare:

> Since I have joined politics, I have become poor. I
> cannot save anymore. Well, before I could really save.
> My husband often asks me what I do with my salary.
> You spend money all the time and you are broke. I
> cannot tell him [my husband] that somebody came
> to ask me for some money (from direct conversation
> with Oumou Sankare, August 2007).

There is a serious divergence about the argument of politics being equal to personal profit among African women. The majority of the constituencies believe that their leaders are wealthy based on their political leadership position. They can hardly understand that there are some leaders who are not wealthy. On the other hand, what is significant on the political scene in Africa is that the majority of women join the political scene at a time when they have an unenviable economic situation or they are solicited by male politicians. These same women become easy targets for unscrupulous politicians and the transaction leadership system they put in place. A woman, who becomes conscientized about the politics of injustices, has to fight against all sorts of adversities in order to serve the people with equality and fairness.

Women and Political Adversities

This sections amply deals with the forces that either hinder women's political participation or discourage their political leadership based on social, economic, religious, or gender issues. Among debates about women's political involvement, political adversity is one of the arguments that are present in most of the women's political discourse. Women activists such Mrs Sira Diop, Aminata Dramane Traore, Najatu Mohammad, Wangari Maathai, Bernadette Lahai and others discussed how political activities had been controlled by men and the local customs, with various ramifications in state structures. Women have played tremendous roles in keeping families and communities together (Bennett, 2014) in the peace process, but they are today on the political sidelines. Women activists identify the root of their social and political invisibility is the fact that men are the main actors on the political scene. It seems that men enjoy women's non-participation in political activities and use social customs and religion as arguments to disqualify women from the political leadership positions. Concomitantly, if men are considered to be a handicap to women's political integration or advancement, women are also seen as playing an important role in this lack of progress that they are experiencing. From a conversation with Dado, she discussed that:

Well, I met only one problem. You know us women; we do not like each other. We are the reason for our own failures. I was elected by a political party and I left that party to join another political party because of jealousy. I told those women that election will decide between us. We will see who has constituencies and who does not have constituencies. When I tried to run for reelection for a second term, women in one of the political parties were not happy. They did not want me to go back to the city hall. They even told me *I ju, a ju te toro an ka meri la tuguni* (she will not put down her butt in our city hall again). I said ok. I was the leader of my group. They said that I am renting a house, I am not from Bamako, and I do not have a constituency. I said yes I did not have constituencies but I was elected for my first term by a political party (August 2007).

The argument of certain women about their political failure is very often described as a rivalry that is sometimes orchestrated by male politicians. Male politicians manipulate some women to defy other women on a personal basis. Knowing that certain attacks can be devastating to the political sense, opponents never equivocate using negative terminologies to oust their opponents from the political race. The same hostility, as explained by certain women in the political scene, is very often used as a source of discouragement of most women's political activism. Conversely, there are women activists who use the same adversity as an argument for their political involvement, source of inspiration, and motivation in politics that they use to their own advantage. This passage of Dado is a flagrant testimony of those women who accept to make the sacrifice despite the risks.

I told them what you said is true that I do not have a house, I am not from Bamako, I have no constituency but I will remove people from Bamako from their seat and take their position. In Bamanankan (Bamanan)

> *ne ye jatigi faa yiri de ye. Ne ta ye o ye. N'ko an bɛ nyɔgɔn na sa.* (I am someone who kills his/her host. That is what I do. I say, we are at war). [This literally means that she is ingrate]. That is what I am, and the fight is on now. They did all they could. I fought to become the first candidate on the list of my political party. In the city hall, I was only the fourth woman on the list (from direct conversation with Dado, August 2007).

The risk political leaders confront on the political scene is seen as a double dilemma that may come from the counterpart men or even from the women themselves. Furthermore, it is the unfriendly action of some women that many women political leaders are engaged to combat. In general, African women political leaders sometimes tend to forget that a politician is a public figure that is subject to all sorts of attacks and has no privacy.

> At the beginning of my political career, I could not speak before people. I was ashamed. Even now, I happen to have those moments. In politics, people say all sorts of things about you. They call you names, people who should not insult you or speak to you (from direct conversation with Oumou Sankare, August 2007).

The impact of personal attack on women leaders has engendered political discontent and discouragement and has at the same time reduced the number of women to vie for political leadership positions. Even though women believe in the necessity of their presence in the leadership positions, the dynamism that they nourish the early hours of the democratic event has considerably reduced. This downfall in politics is explained by the attack on the structure of the family, in which both parents are the pillars. In the Malian society, calling someone's parents' names is a way to disqualify or declare a merciless war with such a person. The pulling out of certain women from the political scene is explained or justified by the severity or the gravity of the affront someone receives from other competitors.

The difficulties or fears most women on the political scene face in Mali have been mainly personal attacks they have received from other women. Oumou Sankare insists on the danger of that personal attack from some women in these words "there are times they insult you". Oumou Sankare was astonished by the ferociousness of certain women toward other women. She wondered if it was the same women that solicit her to become their leaders. According to Oumou Sankare, there was no irregularity committed during her candidacy that could explain certain attitudes of other women toward her.

> Me, the way I was chosen was that I had a meeting with a group of women, they said during the meeting that Oumou it is necessary to set a policy for the association. And they elected me as the leader of the group. It was the same women who called my parents' names before everyone. I was attacked by a woman for the fact that me, I was chosen. It was that woman who came to me and stated that Oumou it is necessary to make the policy for the group. There were times I remained silent and disoriented. I was not the only one in this case; some other people were attacking everyone (from direct conversation with Oumou Sankare, August 2007).

Generally, when followers are not satisfied with the leadership due to a failure to put their will into action, such as a personal interest, they engage a merciless adversity in order to manifest their discomfort. It turns out that they are leaders who are not awarded the realities on the political scene and what may happen at times of frustration. Such leaders are either not ready to make the sacrifice or find the political scene unfriendly. The absence of commitment and the realities of the political field lead some women to resign from their leadership positions that they find not worth their energy and time. A political scene experience, such as Oumou Sankare's with people that "insulted [her] father and [her] mother in front of everyone", would be likely to discourage many women who hold parents sacred. In the Malian society, parents deserve special respect and no matter how hard the degree of conflict between two people is, they are not supposed to show disrespect to each other's parents. The lack of morality from some people on the political scene is considered by many politicians as an absence of manners and self-respect that should not be an integral part of politics.

In addition to the animosity in politics, there are also the economic aspects that some politicians find unmanageable:

> Since I have joined politics, me, I became poor. I cannot save any more money. Before, I was able to save some money. My husband often asks me, what do you do with your salary?

> You do not pay food or bills, but you are always poor. I cannot tell him that somebody came to ask me for some money (from direct conversation with Oumou Sankare, August 2007).

In contrast to the widespread perception of corrupt politicians enriching themselves from state coffers, several women argue that even if you are rich when you join the political scene, your wealth begins to fade away due to constituents who constantly ask for favors or gifts. Politics in this context mislead some women into expecting or having the understanding of politics being one thing, which does not match the reality of the scene. Based on such an experience, many women prefer to withdraw themselves from politics even though they vied for their political positions. Some other women argue that their experience on the political scene forces them to abandon politics losing the taste they had acquired for politics.

The expression in Bamanankan *a ju te toro an ka meri la tuguni* means "she will not put down her bottom in our city hall again" is seen as a lack of respect between people that declare upon each other a furious fight. Based on the reality of the political scene, some women find unbearable to vie for political seats with people they consider outsiders. The animosity in politics fueled by certain leaders does not help women that are the minority in the political leadership position. Another element in this argument is the work of men politicians. Most of the women argued that such hostility between women is a work of men. According to women activists such as Najatu Mohammad, it is the same men that use religion to reinforce their position in the family and subordinate women's political participation to the will of their husbands. Observing a Moslem society, mainly in Mali, women think they need to have the approval of their spouse before engaging in any political activity. In this context, man is supposed to be the head of the family and the bread winner. He is viewed as the only decision maker in the household and the wife owes him respect for her salvation, according to the interpretation by certain men. Referring to the religious argument, there is no such absolute power given to men by the Muslim religion as the head of the family according to Najatu Mohammad. She argued that whenever the Almighty Allah talks about men he talks about women as well, and that there is no heaven called men heaven or women heaven (2010).

Following these arguments, the majority of women have witnessed certain rights taken away from them based on the social customs that prevent them to be in the public arena. What women denounce is the fact that they are encouraged or applauded on the public scene whenever it fits the interests of men. Different interpretations of Mali's primary religion, Islam, are employed by both men and women on the political scene to either encourage or to discredit women's participation alongside men in public life. The collaboration between men and women on the political scene is interpreted in different forms but it turns out that it always plays at the disadvantage of women. Finally, most of the women interviewed also criticize the social customs that reinforce the power of men over women by constraining women's movements in society, as discussed by Dado:

> Well, you know that politics is difficult based on the
> realities, mainly religion. The first thing is when you

are a politician, people see in you a depraved woman. People think that once you are involved in politics you are available for anyone. That is the first thing people think about me when I started politics and then that they solicited me to become a member of a political party x office, I was in Paris. My husband called me that x and x came to see me and wanted you to become a member of their party. He said that he accepted their proposition with its advantages and disadvantages. Because occupying a political seat, people call you all the time. You can stay at the meeting up to two or three o'clock in the morning. You travel all the time. Well, for a married woman, some husbands do not understand. I told him if you accepted their proposition with its consequences there is no problem for me. From that day on, I felt at ease in my family with my husband. And at any time when they come to me, there is no problem. They can come and tell me tomorrow you are traveling; I get ready and leave. Sometimes my husband is not at home I write a message for him. Truly I have not had problems (with her husband) (from direct conversation with Dado, August 2007).

The fact that a spouse gives his opinion about his wife's political and social participation should not per se make the wife a subordinate in the family. The same is also possible in many African countries to have a wife give her opinion about her husband's political and societal activities. However, the stereotypes women face as politicians have neither facilitated their work nor encouraged them to join politics. It is, therefore, difficult to say that all women encounter this labeling during their political career, but many women are unfortunate to go through this experience in politics. Women realize that they have to engage in a fight, that needs sometimes needs to be done alone, as discussed by Bell Hooks (2000) in the introductory page of her book *Feminist Theory: From Margin to Center*: "Many of us live in circumstances and environments where we must engage in feminist fight alone."[81] When there is an urgency of action, it sometimes becomes time-consuming to wait for collective action. It is during such a time of crises that leaders emerge and demarcate themselves by their passion, sense of responsibility and risk taking (Burns 1978).

One of the difficulties women politicians face in Africa is the relationship with the constituencies that are in daily need of support or help from the leader. Women sometimes think that they spend more time with their constituencies rather than with their own family, which exposes them to criticism from their husbands and others:

> Well, before my door was always closed. Since I became a politician, people go all the time to see me at home. My hostile husband did not like that. After a period of observation, he told me even if a little boy comes to see you, you will accompany him to the door. I told him that those little boys, whom you see, are voters. Well, yesterday evening when I came home they told me that there was a militant of my political party who wanted to run for a political position. He left and another one came. I went to discuss a little bit with that militant. The militant left there was another woman who came that I do not know with her request. For example, when the party makes the loincloths, you cannot give it to everyone. The ones, who receive the loincloth, are happy and vote for you, but those, who did not receive it, will not vote for you. It is based on these similar situations that me, I am a little discouraged. My husband does not like much politics even though he was the one to encourage me in the beginning when I was afraid to go to political meetings. But now he complains that I am all the time outside and that I do not have time for him and the children anymore (from direct conversation with Oumou Sankare, August 2007).

---

[81]   Bell Hooks (2000). Feminist Theory: From Margin to Center. Pluto Press

Many women in public life find it difficult to address the concerns of their husbands regarding their careers, perhaps because the men experience insecurity about their roles when their wives become public figures. However, if some women political leaders are more concerned about the complaints and the impact on their children because of their political activism, some other women believe that women need to remain on the political scene despite the consequences. The stumbling block for women's political involvement is poignantly discussed by Mrs Djire:

> For example, we happened to spend the night out during the municipal election. Will all men accept that? They do not accept that, and also they do not like every time we go to meetings. They do not accept. There are many men who do not accept that. They refuse. There are also women who cannot confront their husband. If I say confront, if it is not in mutual agreement, it will become a war (from direct conversation with Mrs. Djire, August 2007).

Indeed, in order for women to experience, enjoy, and participate in political activities, they have to challenge their husbands and that is not always an easy task, based on the social customs. It is the same customs that secure the position of men in the family.

Another reason for men's insecurity can be explained by the role African women have supposedly played in breaking the bond between relatives, as stated by Rosaldo: "Men work to bind lineage mates together; women work to tear them apart."[82] In certain African societies, women work to ensure the progress of her husband and sons while men are required to work for collective progress. Even though this statement can be challenged, it deserves certain credibility in human society. In fact, what is not mentioned in this statement is that most of those women refuse to play peripheral roles in the family they moved to. The attitude of men vis-à-vis women's political

---

[82]   Rosaldo, M. Z; Lamphere, L; Bamberger, J. (1974). Woman, culture, and society. Stanford University Press. p92

activism has been considered sometimes beneficial and sometimes disadvantageous for women's political progress. Bintou Sidibe has very often drawn people's attention to the hardship between women politicians and in their respective families. If women seem enthusiastic joining political leadership positions, this enthusiasm is very often cut short and is instrumental to political exploitation of some politicians.

> We cannot tell you that there is no problem because between us sometimes, there is exclusion. What they like is to manipulate people. We, the women constitute the weakest link. They use us for a moment and then get rid of us and look for a new group that is easy to manipulate. Thus, there is a problem. They tried to keep me aside and I did not understand. There had been so many things going on, they composed the bureau without me, I did not say anything since I was elected. I had a right to membership, I was attending meetings. But, in the long run I was again integrated. They manipulated women's elections at the high level during the election of their bureau. They removed me, but they did not know that was not my aims. Because, I said at the beginning that I will not go to the conference, I will not be a staff member. But, some people asked me to stay and to seize any opportunity. Thus, for that reason I agreed to go to the conference. They chose people they trusted. But, that did not work for anybody; the Bureau finally did not work. It turns out that I positioned myself in the base. They did everything to bring people and it did not work.

> It was not a personal choice; there was someone who orchestrated the whole thing so that I can be on the political scene. In politics, they try to target people especially women who have a lot of followers. They choose those people as the pillar and try to have enough constituencies (from direct conversation with Bintou Sidibe, August 2007).

The experience of Bintou Sidibe is similar to many other women politicians in Africa. The survival of these women in politics relies on their own tenacity to prevail before any adversity. If some women argue the strong presence of men in their activities, other women accuse women's lack of political experience. The massive presence of men in women's activities can be explained by the argument of Najatu Muhammad in these following terms: 'Men normally perceive women as irrational, apolitical, emotional, and incapable of taking right decisions' (2010, 7th annual Trust Dialogue in Abuja). These women argue that when men elect their political bureau women do not interfere, but when it is the time for women to elect the members of their bureau, men do everything to manipulate that election. Certain women say that men could go to the extreme in looking for women elsewhere to elect as leaders. Another observation is that men sometimes use some women to fight those who are in the leadership position and are no longer willing to cooperate. The conscientized women later realize that they have been for a long time defending a counterproductive agenda that does not benefit women. A number of women activists argue against the fact women are engaged in the political scene to combat their sisters. In the same token, Mrs. Djire draws people's attention to the problem among men in the political sphere to be virulent although they know how to keep their disagreement silent.

> We often complain, we say that there is no solidarity among women. It is worse with men. But, they have debates of ideas, to fight one another after that one sees nothing. But for women, people can see them fighting. Me, my voters are especially women. With the women, I do not have much problem. They are the majority of people who help me. With men, it is a little more complicated. It is especially the adult men who have problems with women. When it is time to renew the staff of the political party, women generally do not intervene (from direct conversation with Mrs. Djire, August 2007).

The lack of fairness between political actors tend to create discomfort among women vis-à-vis their counterpart men. Women poignantly argue that there is no transparency in the way men handle political affairs and most of the time they disqualify women from vying for political leadership positions. Men in this context are the undeniable obstacle for women's political promotion. Moreover, the obstacle of women on the political scene, according to certain women, is not only caused by men but the education system that they inherited from the colonial oppressive system that gave all power to men.[83] After the departure of the colonial oppressive forces, African states struggled to organize life in a way that could be beneficial for their individual societies. It is in part many people in the African continent tend to believe that women have no political history, but men have timidly tried to fill the gap after the departure of the colonial oppressors by initiating women to politics, despite some gains during the fight for independence. Based on these arguments, African women believe that there is a great responsibility of their men in their political backwardness. Based on women's arguments, men are the main part of the obstacles to the promotion of women. They believe that this factor has been existing since the beginning of their political history in the continent.

There are also longstanding social forces at play. For some women, boys go to school while young girls do not go to school. Adult men are connected to the world news and they are connected to the outside world. Women stay home whereas men are everywhere with their different friends discussing issues related to politics. Men listen to the radio and read newspapers on top of what they have been trained to become at school. Thus, from early socialization through adult norms of behavior, women and men have different behavior, reactions, and vision toward politics. Men in general educate themselves politically by looking for information, and they train themselves politically. Educated women, even those who have higher degrees, do not reach the level of men in political

---

[83]   Shor, I, (1992). Empowering Education: Critical Teaching for Social Change. University of Chicago Press.

involvement. Thus, men tend to have greater preparation for and greater experience in politics, and some women recognize that the invitation or assistance of men is necessary for their involvement, as for Mrs. Djire:

> If it was not men asking women to join the political scene, it was going to be difficult for women to join politics on their own because we are not used to politics. If in the beginning women were going to school, they would have been well trained, and there would have been no problem for them about politics (from direct conversation with Mrs. Djire, August 2007).

Having paved the way to political leadership for women, men continue to take advantage of women based on their influence in the society. In order to explain this dichotomy between women and men in politics in Africa, it is important to identify the different parameters that come into play. There are many factors that play against African women's political and social lighting up, which are rooted in the existence of several societies in the continent. The juxtaposition of things such as running a household in general, a job (if she has a job), and the society she lives in, limit women to fully enjoy a public role. There is also the position of the husband; in which many husbands do not accept that their wives leave the house to stay late away from the family even though such behavior is tolerated or accepted by a minority of married men in African societies. And those women, who happened to have benefit of such behavior, are very often called emancipated, divorced, or modern women. According to Nicolas:

> The woman who has succeeded in freeing herself of the family yoke and has overcome certain taboos, a woman who lives on her own and who therefore is more likely to choose for herself the husband who suits her (Nicolas, 1967. p.59).

Women of such persuasion are repeatedly called names and most of the time have difficulty being accepted by men, and they are very often feared by the rest of women based on the social principles. In many African countries, for a woman to choose a husband, that suits her without the blessing of the family, is not a good sign for the couple. And this attitude vis-à-vis women creates a trepidation that has resonance with their political contribution.

The fear of women toward their sisters in politics has its ramification in their political history paved by men politicians. Even though several women politicians believe that they are in politics to support or help every day women, the sporadic fight between women on the political scene has never facilitated their own political advancement. Women on the political scene generally formulate their political difficulties as instrumental due to men's actions and fail to mention the fight they engage in with each other when they vie for political positions. Even though many women on the political scene claim to support women candidates, they still continue to see them as their competition. Mrs. Djire talks below about her experience with her fellow women on the political scene:

> We were about 400 candidates. We were two women on the list of the candidates, and we were selected. And those who were not selected tried get rid of us (from direct conversation with Mrs. Djire, August 2007).

This phenomenon in the political sphere mainly between women is not uncommon as described by several women. On the other hand, some women in leadership positions have tried to be critical toward their real obstacle in politics; they argue that women themselves can be serious threats to other women. Based on these arguments about politics, several women discussed that they had no desire to occupy a political leadership position based on the fact that they thought politics for them was not an easy task. They would rather observe politicians fighting each other for positions. Importantly, however, some women escaped from these adversities for the reason that they were either solicited by the people or a political party based on their influence in the community. These are the common words heard from many woman politicians in Mali, such as Oumou Sankare:

> I am the chair of women movement of my district.
> They even came to me at home to become the chair
> of the sub-branch of our political party (from direct
> conversation with Oumou Sankare, August 2007).

Many women seize the opportunity and join a political party of their choice that they find more appealing to them.

Although men have been for a long time considered the main oppressor of women on the political scene, some women believe that men have supported women. In many societies, such as in Africa, religion and tradition have given men the duty to provide for the women even though she earns a monthly salary at the end of the month. Men are always considered the main breadwinner; however, this tendency is disappearing today due to the changes in modern African societies. The responsibility of men to provide for the family is still active in certain societies in Mali as supported by Mrs. Djire:

> ...many people who went on early retirement and
> did not succeed. That was caused by the problem of
> salary; woman-teachers did not have salary problems
> because their husbands were providing for them. It did
> not affect them in their family. And it did not affect
> anything in our household (from direct conversation
> with Mrs. Djire, August 2007).

After women get married in many African societies, men are then considered the head of the family and he is supposed to provide for the family's needs. These customs explain why women were not suffering for a nonpayment of their salary at the end of the month.

Generally, in many families in Mali, especially a Moslem one, a woman is not supposed to provide for the family's daily needs, this is considered to be the responsibility of men. Based on this fact, a married woman is not supposed to experience financial hardship unless the spouse is unemployed. Despite the economic condition a husband experiences, he still has the obligation to provide for his wife and for the education of the children.

The recent increase in the number of women in political leadership positions has its origin in different domains such as young girls' education and some tolerance of social customs vis-à-vis young girls or women's participation in certain social activities that has importantly advantaged women today. Bintou insists that the difficulty women have in politics is related to their small number in leadership positions. In order for women to make a change, they need to have a majority in politics, which is not the case as Bintou discussed:

> Women are not the majority in politics, in decision-making. It is men who are the majority on this ground (from direct conversation with Bintou, August 2007).

Even when women do lead in politics, there may be discord between leaders and constituencies over the elected person's responsibilities to the group. Changes or problems in the leader's personal life may damage others' perception of her work:

> I hear people saying that they no longer see me at meetings. They say I used to go to women group meetings and they do not see me anymore. I said how you can you see me! I felt sick right after the elections. I spent three years confined in the house. I spent about three years very sick. They did not understand that; if not what do I benefit here (meaning working at the city hall). I benefit nothing from here in the city hall that could keep me away if it was not lately (from direct conversation with Bintou, August 2007).

Opinions are divided on the performance of women leaders in office. Many women argue that once their leaders are appointed to a public office, they begin to forget or even neglect the rest of the group. Such statement is never taken lightly by women political leaders; for them this attitude of their constituencies is a misunderstanding of politics. Women leaders continue to argue that just the simple word 'political office' is misleading people and making them believe that people in political offices can perform miracles. With such a mindset about politics, people tend to distance themselves from political responsibilities leaving them in the hand of the sole elected people. It turns out that those elected people see that as an opportunity to political laissez aller and laissez faire; hence an instrument of corruption. Even though there might be some realities in the suspicions the women groups have towards their leaders in the continent, it is not always the case that 'power corrupts and absolute power corrupts absolutely' (Knowles 2006) (57). Conversely, some leaders think that certain people's negativity is merely based on the benefit they gain from their leaders once appointed to a public office. And based on the personal experiences of certain women leaders, they cogitate that their fellow women tend to forget the realities of their own social values whenever personal interest is concerned.

Some women leaders believe that there is a misconception about political office that many followers see as a place that corrupts and distances leaders from the people. The personal story of Bintou is a tangible proof of disconnection between the leaders and the followers:

> You see, I said that we do not benefit anything from here that can keep me forgetting whatsoever. That is what the people do not understand. On top of that, I just lost my husband. (Religious constraint that keep women from the political scene). The widowhood and everything were over four months. You do not go out, you do not attend events. Me, I am obliged to disappear. *U t'o olu si famuya* they do not understand any of those things (from direct conversation with Bintou, August 2007).

The story of Bintou is a tangible example of the misunderstanding between leaders and their constituencies. The lack of a clear understanding of certain women about politics makes the task difficult for women in public offices that are constantly eager to help out other women or anybody who solicits their help. This attitude of women on the political scene as discussed by Solheim has been defined by many political leadership experts as a nurturing, collaborative, empathetic and sensitive style in politics.[84] These leadership characteristics displayed by women on the political scene are considered to be important leadership tenets even though some seem to consider this style with reserve arguing that there is no such difference between women and men leadership on the political scene. The difference here on the political scene is explained by the long time experience of men in political affairs that continues to intimidate some women, while lighting a fire under others, like Oumou:

> Women have sometimes inferiority complex before men. Me, I know that I am not going to give up my position for a man because he is a man. I am going to fight; I will not give up my position. It is not because I am a woman that I let a man take my position (from direct conversation with Oumou, August 2007).

Oumou strongly believes that men's attitudes on the political scene toward women cannot intimidate her and that she is willing to make the sacrifice in order to remain in the leadership position. In the same vein, Bernadette Lahai, a Liberian politician, attested in a conversation with Cady that: "One of the problems facing women in the enjoyment of their rights is the access to justice."[85] These rights of women on the political scene are mainly centered

---

[84] Solheim, B. O. (2006). On Top of the World: Women's Political Leadership in Scandinavia and Beyond. Greenwood Publishing Group
[85] Video produced by Anna Cady () Pathways of Women's Empowerment 2012. A Real World Film. Retieved December, 12 2014 from https://www.youtube.com/watch?v=WodVLq8YRv8

on fair representation of women in the leadership position, hence in the government. Some women argue that the adversity that women very often face vis-a-vis men is originated from the fear men have for women joining the political scene to vie for political leadership positions. As Lahai continues in her conversation with Cady, she said:

> When you start seeing men, you know putting all of these roadblocks, you know against women they use that as a way you know of hide sometimes their inefficiencies. But if you are confident, you only see the presence of women as complementing.

In general, most women political leaders do not consider themselves as absolute authorities, and they try to remain in constant contact with the followers and work with them hand in glove. This work of women on the political scene is seen as a way to demystify politics by breaking away from all sorts of social taboos as Lahai underlined (Mirsky and Radlett 2000).

> The key thing really important for us…is to have your family support. In order to reach the goal of making political scene family friendly, some women politicians argued toward the responsibility of men, that men should not be daunted by the presence of women as attests this passage: men of quality are not afraid of equality.[86]

Even as political leadership starts to open up to women, some men are still skeptical about the presence of women, due to the fact that they do not know much about the type of leadership women try to bring on the political arena. However, the presence of women in politics in the African continent today needs to be seen as beneficial first to women and then to the whole continent and the multiparty democratic system.

---

[86] Mirsky, J., Radlett, M. (2000). No Paradise Yet: The World's Women Face the New Century. Zed books. UK.777. p95

In general, the adversities African women are facing today on the political scene are twofold contingent on attitudes that the majority of women cannot demarcate themselves from the status quo established in politics. As a consequence, women leaders motivate those at the grassroots level to vote for the sole women candidates. Many women tend to solve their political hardship by casting their vote for women candidates even though they do not know much about the candidate(s). In addition, a disadvantaged economic situation pushed many women to express their discontent by joining the political scene. Equally, it is the conception of many women about political leadership that continues to encumber various women's political aspirations. Rose Mensah-Kutin from the ABANTU for Development explains:

> Originally when you think of a leader you think of a very big person, you think of somebody who has to be obeyed, you think of a leader also in masculine terms. And so immediately women [in Ghana] feel that that is not a space for them and they are also made to feel that way.[87]

These preconceived ideas of women about political leadership intimidate them and can further keep women away from the political scene and to vie for leadership positions. As a consequence, women continue to experience the same phenomena today they used to experience in the past even though there is little improvement today. The irony in this case is that women are used on the political scene to fight other women to the benefit of men. If some women take pleasure in working in the racket of men, it is to understand that some other women demonstrate their opposition to this work of men. The willingness of certain women to support women activists explains their opposition to the discriminating attitudes of men. African women are most of the time limited in their action because

---

[87] Dzodzi Tsikata and Akosua K. Darkwah from the Pathways of Women's Empowerment: What are we Learning? Conference, 20 – 24 January 2009.

of the role men play in their life. This following statement of a woman patient to her doctor who is a political activist explains the duality between certain political leaders and their constituencies. As the patient attests in these terms that "we have all receive the order to fight you...I don't know how we could do it for...your husband is the sole doctor here and you are sole nurse here"[88]. It is not only on the political scene that politicians are unaware of the adversity they face rather their ambition or their dedication and sense of sacrifice that make them face adversities are sometimes considered forlorn.

Many African women have for a long time a preconceived model of a leader regardless their degree of education, which continues to be a handicap even though they are playing a leadership role in their everyday lives.

Women as Political Leaders

The argument of women in this section deals with the long presence of women in politics and that they are not political novices doing politics on the periphery. Paying attention to the different definitions of leadership and seeing the roles played by women in their individual communities and organizations, it would be difficult to deny the leadership role they have been playing. Even though leadership has mainly been considered for a long time gender oriented by several experts, the existence of leadership attributes has always been the domain of women.[89] Many of the African women I talked to define their leadership skills based on their everyday role they play within the family and community organizations. They argue that in these roles, they should be considered as qualified leaders. Importantly, women rarely doubt their ability to mobilize people around a common objective, and that is considered as a habitual past time for most woman politicians interviewed. They discuss

---

[88]   Dzodzi Tsikata and Akosua K. Darkwah from the Pathways of Women's Empowerment: What are we Learning? Conference, 20 –

[89]   Solheim, B. O. (2006). On Top of the World: Women's Political Leadership in Scandinavia and Beyond. Greenwood Publishing Group

their involvement in politics as based on their intrinsic value in the society, which makes them significant targets for political parties. One of the leadership attributes discussed by Bintou attests those aforementioned arguments.

> I can mobilize people well. I can mobilize people well; at first I had a group of eighty women before I joined the political scene. I organize *tontines* which allow me to see them [women] very often. And ever since I have been on the political scene. (From direct conversation with Bintou, August 2007).

Based on the testimony of many women's political involvement, it is motivating to hear their stories about the leadership role they play or used to play within associations. Most of the women that I had the chance to converse with or analyzed their political leadership, argued in favor of politics helping women to change. The emphasis that women have on their organizations help them remediate some of their social situations even though the main goal for some woman leaders is to create a bond between women within the same community. It is the competencies displayed on those different scenes that make women important targets or potential politicians. Many women politicians such as Oumou explained her political involvement based on her own experience with women's associations. Her argument in this sense is that politicians, mainly men, base their political calculus on how to have many constituencies among women. The main intention in this calculus is to gain the support of a woman's association leader to join a target party. Gaining the support of a leader, politicians try in this way to have the target group adhere to a political party as discussed:

> We have organized the women in a sense that every month we can be together and meet in one of the member's house and contribute to put money together. It is because I was the chairperson of an association of woman that people have solicited me. I believe it

was based on my position in the association that they can say I have followers. And they say to themselves if they happen to make the leader join their party, they will have the support of her followers. I believe it was because of that (the leadership role) (from direct conversation with Oumou Sankare, August 2007).

However, motivating women within an association or an organization to support a political candidate has hardly benefited women in their struggle for political leadership. It is rather a way to distract women, to diverge their attention from things that matter to them and that they find worthwhile to discuss. As an example, which has been discussed by some women, questions about the bank of grains (a system established by the Malian government to stock grains and sell them back cheaply to people who have a very low income during difficult periods of the year) are important topics for mothers that experience food scarcity during the season before the harvest (May, June, and July). Such an issue concerning family welfare happens to attract many women's attention on the political scene. Nevertheless, this statement about women rarely negates the fact that some women leaders are concerned about bringing their fellow women to defend a common cause.

If the majority of women in Africa have found politics being a past time for men and their unique domain, this trend is rapidly changing today based on women's awareness of politics and the involvement of local and international organizations. Today, there are an increasing number of women ready to engage in a fight on the political scene in order to make their voices heard. Before, they were considered the silenced group due to their number and their absence on the political scene, however, the number of African women in political leadership positions are gradually increasing. Even though their progress is considered by many political experts less significant, the inactivity of African women in politics seems to belong to the past. This observation of political experts is mainly based on the leadership role women currently play on the political scene.

CONCLUSION

• •

Women revealed that their experience in politics is that power on the political scene remains in the hands of men politicians instead of being equally shared between men and women, even as women make some inroads into political life. Several situations indicated by women help illustrate this phenomenon in the African continent, mainly on the Malian political scene. One of the examples is the disadvantage women inherited from education rooted in the Western colonial oppression that gave men a natural right of access to education and political power. In addition, the advent of the new multiparty democratic system in the continent has not played a major role to change this trend. Even though the role of the international donors' influence is considered to be the driving force behind women's political emancipation, it is not always seen as positive in many African countries.

Another argument is the misinterpretation of the ideals of democracy by men and women politicians that sometimes brings conflicts, which is a key component of misunderstanding between political actors. In addition, the role played by foreign governments to support and encourage the participation of women in politics in the African continent without trying to find a solution to the different causes that hinder women's political activism become a problem, in introducing new systems that are at the same time new and confusing for both women and men politicians.

Furthermore, women's political leadership is still at its debut and needs expertise from men that have been on the political scene for a long time as the history of political leadership attests. The opportunity is given to women today to vie for political positions with men and that still does not give the women much room to access leadership positions in Africa. Women that occupy leadership positions, give the impression of being less significant in politics and very often play peripheral roles. Then there are some women that see political opportunity as a way to compete with their counterpart men and not an occasion for women to use their own expertise for the political prospect.

However, despite the quid pro quo created around politics, women's presence on the political scene in Africa has brought a tremendous change in their social life and has given women an opportunity to bring their competence to political leadership. In addition, the number of women in political leadership is increasing gradually, not only on the African continent, but also elsewhere in the world where women have less voice to be heard on the political and social scene. Thus, women's experiences represented in this work can help provide an understanding of the form of leadership that women would like to have in the political sphere.

REFERENCES

Amponsah, N. A., Falola. T (2012). *Women's Roles in Sub-Saharan Africa.* Greenwood Publication. Santa Barbara, California.

Niane, D. T. (Jan 1, 1971). Sundiata: An Epic of Old Mali (Soundjata ou l'epopee mandingue). French Edition.

Gisela G. Geisler (2004). Women and the Remaking of Politics in Southern Africa: Negotiating Autonomy, incorporation and representation. Nordiska Africainstitutet publication

Mandela, W. "The African Woman and Politics". *The 7 th annual Trust Dialogue in Abuja.* 30 July, 2014. http://www.youtube.com/watch?v=hNyaXVD1bRQ

Rose Mensah-Kutin. "Discussing the Women's Manifesto in Ghana". capacity4dev.eu. 21 july 2014. http://www.youtube.com/watch?v=-JVd3fOO188

Bâ, A. H. (1984). Amkoullel, l'enfant peul [The Fulani child]. France: Actes Sud.

Bâ, A. H. (1994). Aspects de la civilisation Africaine: Personne culture et religion. [Aspects of African civilization: people, culture, religion]. France: Présence Africaine.

Bâ, A. H., Gaetani, R. (2008). A Spirit of Tolerance: The Inspiring Life of Tierno Bokar. World Wisdom, Inc.

Bâ, A. H., Taylor, A. P. (1999). The fortunes of Wangrin. Indiana University Press.

Bass, B. M. (1990). From transactional to transformational leadership: Learning to share the vision. Organizational Dynamics, 18, 19-31.

Breitman, G. (1966). Malcolm X speaks: Selected speeches and statements. New York, NY: Grove Press.

Burns J. M. (1978). Leadership. New York, N.Y: Harper & Row.

Darder, A. (2002). Reinventing Paulo Freire: a pedagogy of love. Westview Press.

Darder, A., Baltodano, M., Torres, R. D. (2002). The critical pedagogy reader. Falmer Press, New York

Dewey, J. (1916). Democracy and education. NY: Dover Publications.

Chamberlin, J. (1997). A working definition of empowerment. Spring 1997 vol. 20 No 4. Retrieved September 15, 2009, from http://www.manitoba.cmha.ca/data/1/rec docs/1099 a%20 working%20definition%20of%20empowerment.pdf

Foster, W. P. (1989). Towards a critical practice of leadership. In J. Smythe (Ed.), Critical perspectives on leadership, (pp. 39-62). London, UK: Falmer Press.

Mamdani, M. (1996). Citizen and subject: Contemporary Africa and the legacy of late colonialism. Princeton, NJ: Princeton University Press.

Mazrui, A. A., & Mazrui A. (1998). The power of Babel: Language & governance in the African experience. Chicago: University of Chicago Press.

Babacar Ndiaye. B; Ndiaye. W (2006). *Présidents et ministres de la République du Sénégal*, Dakar, Senegal.

Shor, I, (1992). Empowering Education: Critical Teaching for Social Change. University of Chicago Press.

Okolo M. S. C. (2013). African Literature as Political Philosophy. Published by Zed Books Ltd Retrieved December 12, 2009, from http://eric.ed.gov/ERICWebPortal/custom/portlets/ recordDetails/detailmini.jsp? nfpb=true& &ERICExtSearch SearchValue 0=ED359303&ERI CExtSearch SearchType 0=no&accno=

Popper, M. (2005). Leaders who transform society. Westport, CT: Praeger/Greenwood.

Touré, A., Mariko, N'T. (2005). Amadou Hampâté Bâ, homme de science et de sagesse: mélanges pour le centième anniversaire de sa naissance. Kartala.

Rost, J. C. (1991). Leadership for the twenty-first century. (1st ed.). New York, NY: Praeger. Sembene, O. (1988). Camp de Thiaroye. Film [In Wolof and French with English subtitles] Senghor, L. S. (1991). Négritude et humanisme [Blackness and humanisme]. France: Seuil.

Shor. I. (1992). Culture Wars: School and Society in the Conservative Restoration. The University of Chicago Press.

Thoreau, H. D. (1849). Civil disobedience. Retrieved May 18, 2004, from http://www.eserver. org/thoreau/civill. html.

Ulrich, D., Zenger, J., & Smallwood, N. (1999). Results-based leadership. Boston, MA: Harvard Business School Press.

Wolfenstein, E.V. (1967). The revolutionary personality: Lenin, Trotsky, Ghandi. (1st ed.). Princeton, NJ: Princeton University Press.

Benoist (1987) Église et pouvoir colonial au Soudan français. Administrateurs et missionnaires dans la boucle du Niger (1885-1945), Paris, Karthala.

Antonetti, R. (1930). Rapport au Ministre des Colonies, Brazzaville, 11 décembre 1930, Archives du Congo, Aff. Pol. Carton 838, dossier 2.

Augouard, P. P. (Mgr) (1906). Une visite pastorale dans l'Oubangui. Les Missions catholiques, 11 mai-22 juin: 15. 1934 44 années au Congo, Évreux, Société française Imprimerie et Librairie.

Batumeni, V. (1978). Le Matswanisme des origines à nos jours, Thèse de doctorat, Université de Bordeaux III, Ronéo.

Bernault, F. (1996). Démocratie ambiguë en Afrique centrale. Congo Brazzaville-Gabon 1940- 1965, Paris, Karthala.

Benoist, J. R., (1985) Colonisation et évangélisation, Le Caire, Éditions et publications des Pères jésuites en Égypte.

Benoist, J. R. (1987). Église et pouvoir colonial au Soudan français. Administrateurs et missionnaires dans la boucle du Niger (1885-1945), Paris, Karthala.

Benoist, J. R. (1988) « Félix Éboué et les missions catholiques », Communication au colloque sur la Conférence de Brazzaville, in Brazzaville (Janv.-Fév. 1944) aux sources de la décolonisation, Paris, Plon.

Bikoumou, P. s.d. Monseigneur Auguste-Roch Nkounkou, Brazzaville.

Brunschwig, H. (1963). L'Avènement de l'Afrique noire du xixe siècle à nos jours, Paris, Armand Colin.

Cointet, F. (1970). « Lettres à sa famille en 1920 », in C. Coquery-Vidrovitch, Le Congo au temps des compagnies concessionnaires, Paris, Mouton.

Délicat, C. (1993). Les Pères de la Congrégation du Saint-Esprit au Vicariat de Loango 1886- 1958, Thèse de doctorat, Paris, Université de Paris I.

Houchet, J. B. (Père)(1933). Annales des Pères du Saint-Esprit, oct., Paris, Congrégation du Saint-Esprit.

Luchire, F. & Conac, G. (1979). La Constitution de la République française, Paris, Armand Colin/Economica.

Merle, M. (dir). (1967). Les Églises chrétiennes et la décolonisation, Paris, Armand Colin.

Node-Langlois, É. (1974). Mission spiritaine et administration française devant la polygamie au Cameroun de 1916 à 1939, Paris, Diplôme de l'École pratique des hautes études, 6e section.

Somé, M. (1998).« La christianisation des Dagara au Burkina », Revue française d'Histoire d'Outre-Mer, 85 (319): 33-57.

Witte, J. (1924). Un explorateur et un apôtre au Congo français. Mgr Augouard. Ses mots de voyage et sa correspondance, Paris, Émile-Paul.

Witwicki, R. (1995). Marie et l'évangélisation du Congo (1594-1952), Brazzaville, Centre Chaminade.

Denise Bouche.(1966) Les écoles françaises au Soudan à l'époque de la conquête. 1884-1900. Cahiers d'etudes africaines.

Barthélémy, P. (2003). La formation des Africaines à l'École normale d'institutrices de l'AOF de 1938 à 1958. Edition l'E.H.E.S.S.

Chahana TAKIOU (2008). Revelations of Abdoulaye Sékou Sow (II): "How late Prof. Mohamed Lamine Traoré forced me to resigned" (Les révélations de Me Abdoulaye Sékou Sow (II): «Comment feu le Pr Mohamed Lamine Traoré m'a contraint à la démission). L'INDEPENDANT – Date: 08 Septembre 2008

Read more: Mali – History Background – Percent, Schools, French, and Education – State University.com http://education.stateuniversity.com/pages/942/Mali-HISTORY-BACKGROUND. html#ixzz23hOUJshP

King, E.M., Hill, A. M. (1997). Women's education in developing countries: Barriers, benefits, and policies. The World Bank.

Jean-Marie Volet 2007. Women's perception of French colonial life in 19th century Africa: a fascinating universe challenging conventional. Retrieved 9/26/2011 from wisdomhttp://aflit. arts. uwa.edu.au/colonies 19e eng.html

Troubles post-électoraux, Afrique express N° 152,11 septembre 1997

Mme Diakite Sanaba Sissoko, Traoré Salimata Tamboura, Mbam Mamadou Diarra (AMDH) Many Camara, Mrs. Sy, Kadiatou Sy fought against against a dictatorial regime and a unique thought in Mali. http://www.guide2womenleaders.com/Mali.htm

Aminata Dramane Traoré. Une révoltée altermondialiste 21 mai 2008, Bamako (Mali). Propos recueillis par Sadou Yattara et

Anne Perrin retieved 4/15/13 http://www.oecd.org/fr/csao/publications/41682765.pdf

Sweetman, C. (2000) Women and Leadership. Oxfam, GB.

Jamieson, K. H. (1995). Beyond the double bind: women and leadership. Oxford University Press.

Klenke, K. (1996). Women and Leadership: A Contextual Perspective. Springer Publishing Company. New York.

Mali: Sira Diop: « Le fondamentalisme religieux est entrain d'envahir le Mali! » Par Mame Diarra DIOP 27 août 2009 Source Journal du Mali

Trauth., E. M. (2002). Odd girl out: an individual differences perspective on women in the IT profession. Retrieved 9/20/2013 from http://www.eileentrauth.com/uploads/4/6/7/6/4676002/odd girl out.pdf

Mirsky, J., Radlett, M. (2000). No Paradise Yet: The World's Women Face the New Century. Zed books. UK.777

Mme Sira Diop http://www.wluml.org/fr/node/5504 http://www.bamanet.net/index.php/actualite/les-echos/10716-dossier--les-combattantes-de-la-liberte-combat-pour-la-liberte-lengagement-de-la-femme-avant-lindependance.html

Nicolas, J. (1967). Les juments de Dieux': Ritesde possession et condition feminine en pays Hausa (Vallee de Maradi, Niger) ('Horses of Gods': Spirit possession and women's position in a Hausa society [Maradi Valley, Niger]). Paris: Etudes Nigeriennes.

(2010). Femmes d'Afrique, Mémorial de Rufisque. Jamana Edition

Sept 26, 2011Documentary: Wangari Muta Maathai (1940-2011). Production KTN Kenya Bell Hooks (2000). Feminism Is for Everybody. South End Press

Bell Hooks (2000). Feminist Theory: From Margin to Center. Pluto Press

Jean F. O'Barr (1975). Making the Invisible Visible: African Women in Politics and Policy. African Studies Review Vol. 18, No. 3, Women in Africa (Dec., 1975), pp. 19-27. Published by: African Studies Association Ibn Battuta 1351-1353: Journey to West Africa

Sanankoua, B. (2007). Les États-nations face à l'intégration régionale en Afrique: le cas du Mali. Karthala Editions. http://books.google.com/books?hl=en&lr=&id=sekbaR60oGgC&oi=fnd&pg=PA147&dq=Mme+Sira+diop&ots=3uDdkKotRU&sig=M1NK-3Lvug4oWLYJTUAVlLmepFc#v=onepage&q=Mme%20Sira%20diop&f=false

Diarrah, C. O. (1986). *Le Mali de Modibo Keita*. L'Harmattan Editions. Paris.

Tripp, A. M. (2000). *Women and Democracy in Uganda*. University of Wisconsin Press Tripp, A. M. (2001). Women and Democracy: THE NEW POLITICAL ACTIVISM IN AFRICA. Journal of Democracy Volume 12, Number 3 July 2001

Rosaldo, M. Z; Lamphere, L; Bamberger, J. (1974). Woman, culture, and society. Stanford University Press.

Nana Oye Lithur Gender, Poverty and the Millennium Development Goals. Nana Oye Lithur – EWB Conversation 2010. Video Retrieved 7/10/2011 from https://www.youtube.com/watch?v=K-DE-IerHZg

Philip Effiong (2013)1929 and 1946: Nigerian Women Resist Colonial Laws. Retrieved 10/12/2014 from http://www.philip-effiong.com/Southeastern-Nigerian-Women-Revolt.pdf

Kathleen Sheldon (Aug 2013). Women and Colonialism. Oxford Bibliographies in African Studies Publication

Knowles, E. (2006). What They Didn't Say: A Book of Misquotations. Oxford University Press

Solheim, B. O. (2006). On Top of the World: Women's Political Leadership in Scandinavia and Beyond. Greenwood Publishing Group

Dzodzi Tsikata and Akosua K. Darkwah from the Pathways of Women's Empowerment: What are we Learning? Conference, 20 – 24 January 2009.

Bennet, J. (2014). *Toni Morrison and the Queer Pleasure of Ghosts.* Suny Press.

Video produced by Anna Cady (2014) Pathways of Women's Empowerment 2012. A Real World Film. Retieved December, 12 2014 from https://www.youtube.com/ watch?v=WodVLq8YRv8

Barthelemy, P. (2010). *Africaines et diplômées à l'époque coloniale (1918-1957)*

Rennes: Presses Universitaires de Rennes, (coll. Histoire), 2010, 344 p., [préface de Catherine Coquery-Vidrovitch]

Sawadogo, Balguissa. Jacqueline Marie Therese Ki Zerbo. Retrieved 12/18/2017 from http:// www.ecodufaso.com/ jacqueline-marie-therese-ki-zerbo-une-heroine-des-annees-60/

Sow, A. B. (2011) *Political Leadership in the Hand of Teachers: The Type of Leadership Teacher- Politicians Displayed on the Political Scene in Mali.* VDM Verlag Publisher.

Amadou H. Ba, (1980) *Life and the Teaching of Tierno Bokar, the wiseman of Bandiagara* [vie et enseignement de Tierno Bokar, le sage de Bandiagara]. Paris: Le Seuil